What
Auto Mechanics
Don't Want You to Know

WHAT
AUTO MECHANICS
DON'T WANT YOU TO KNOW

Mark Eskeldson

Technews Publishing

Fair Oaks, CA

Library of Congress Catalog Card Number: 94-60760

ISBN: 0-9640560-0-3

Published by
Technews Publishing, a division of Technews Corp.,
7840 Madison Avenue, Suite 185, Fair Oaks, CA 95628

SECOND EDITION

2nd Printing

Manufactured in the United States of America.

Cover Design by Hilber Nelson

DEDICATION

This book is dedicated to honest, highly-educated, professional auto repair technicians across the country who are tired of incompetent and dishonest mechanics giving their industry a bad name.

ABOUT THE AUTHOR

Mark Eskeldson has been involved in the auto repair industry for 21 years. He has worked as a mechanic in independent repair shops and new car dealership service departments, specializing in diagnosis and repair of electrical, driveability, and computer problems on late-model cars. Mark was also involved for two years in training mechanics to diagnose and repair computer control systems.

The author is currently certified by ASE (National Institute for Automotive Service Excellence) and holds a California Smog Check mechanic license. He is also the host of "Shop Talk: America's Radio Car Clinic."

ACKNOWLEDGMENTS

This book would not have been possible without the cooperation of many people. My special thanks to the following agencies for the time they gave in interviews, providing documentation for the undercover stories, and for their outstanding work in policing the auto repair facilities of their counties and states.

ATTORNEYS GENERAL--
Arizona, California, Florida, Minnesota, Missouri, New Jersey, New York, Pennsylvania, Tennessee, Texas, Utah, Washington

CALIFORNIA--
Bureau of Automotive Repair,
Alameda County District Attorney,
El Dorado County District Attorney,
Sacramento County District Attorney,
San Joaquin County District Attorney

ILLINOIS--
WMAQ-TV (Chicago)

LOUISIANA--
New Orleans Better Business Bureau

MICHIGAN--
Bureau of Automotive Regulation,
WJBK-TV (Detroit)

MINNESOTA--
KSTP-TV (St. Paul)

NEVADA--
Department of Consumer Affairs,
Washoe County District Attorney

WISCONSIN--
Department of Justice

Thanks also to the National Institute for Automotive Service Excellence (ASE) for their work in certifying technicians, and to the American Automobile Association (AAA) for their Approved Auto Repair program that provides technician training and helps consumers locate reputable auto repair facilities.

Contents

Introduction

Have you ever taken your vehicle to a repair shop for routine servicing, or for a repair that you thought would be minor, only to receive a phone call with an estimate that was hundreds of dollars more than you anticipated? Have you ever suspected that you were being "ripped-off," but you didn't know what to do about it?

If you answered "yes" to either of these questions, you're not alone; a U.S. Department of Transportation study claimed that approximately 40% of auto repair costs were unnecessary, resulting in consumer losses of about $40 billion per year.

Over the last twenty-one years, I have seen many consumers take their vehicles to incompetent or dishonest repair shops because of advertising or friends' recommendations. Countless people have asked if I thought they had been ripped-off by well-known shops after they ended up paying hundreds of dollars more than the advertised prices. (Since most of those people had gone to shops that were eventually busted, there is a pretty good chance they were victimized.)

It's obvious that far too many vehicle owners do not know how to spot a potential rip-off before it's too late, or how to tell whether a mechanic is highly-skilled or not. If

1

all consumers had this knowledge (and used it), the incompetent and dishonest shops would all disappear because they wouldn't have enough customers to stay in business.

This book was written to give consumers the information they need to avoid becoming victims of incompetent or dishonest repair shops. Commonly-used tactics of unnecessary repair schemes are exposed, and actual examples are given of well-known shops that have been charged with the sale of unnecessary parts and services. Also included are details of the undercover investigations that were used to build cases against those shops.

Tips are also given for locating well-trained, highly-skilled technicians that people can trust. Many vehicle owners spend hundreds (or thousands) of dollars on repairs that aren't necessary, so it's definitely worth the effort that is required to find the best shops. Readers who haven't found a trustworthy shop yet can use this as a reference book--if they're tempted to go to a particular shop because they've seen an ad for low-priced repairs, they can turn to the appropriate chapter for a quick lesson on how to avoid a repair scam.

Last, but not least, readers will learn how "secret warranties" can be used to get free repairs and tricks car salesmen use to make outrageous profits. The information in the last chapter alone could save thousands of dollars on the purchase of a new car or truck!

CHAPTER 1

How Honest
Are Most Mechanics?

In the course of my career as an auto mechanic, I have worked in 6 different repair facilities, along with approximately 80 other mechanics. Two of the facilities were new car dealerships; one was a tire, brake, and front end shop; the other three were independent repair shops. Attending automotive classes and working as a training representative also put me in contact with literally hundreds of other mechanics.

From my experience in the auto repair industry, I would say that most mechanics (at least 80%) are basically honest. What I mean by "basically honest" is that they don't plan ahead of time how they are going to charge people for unnecessary repairs, or for repairs that were not even done.

The remainder (less than 20%) often use unfair or fraudulent business practices, giving honest mechanics a bad name, and should be prosecuted to the full extent of the law. Some of the most-common schemes used to sell unnecessary repairs are described in this chapter and in the chapters covering specific types of repairs.

DISHONEST MECHANICS

There are three basic types of dishonest mechanics. The first type sells a major repair because he honestly believes that it's necessary, but he quickly discovers that the vehicle only needs a minor repair instead. To make sure no one accuses him of charging for work that wasn't done, he does the major repair anyway.

The second type knows in advance that the vehicle only needs a minor repair, but he tells the customer that it needs major repairs anyway. If the customer falls for it, he actually does the major repairs.

The third type will give an estimate for major repairs with no intention of actually doing them. For example, after locating and repairing the transmission part that caused a problem, he paints the transmission to make it look like it was rebuilt. Then he charges the customer for a complete overhaul, even though it wasn't done.

BASICALLY HONEST--BUT INCOMPETENT

Although the average mechanic fully intends to give his customers an honest deal, he often finds himself in situations that force him to choose between telling a lie and losing a lot of money. This situation occurs when a mechanic makes a wrong diagnosis, spending a considerable amount of time working on a vehicle and installing parts that cannot be returned. After all that work, he discovers that the problem is not solved and additional repairs are needed.

If he tells the customer the truth (that he misdiagnosed the problem), he may lose a customer and several hundred dollars; but if he tells the customer a lie (that the work he has already done was necessary, but after he started working on the vehicle he discovered additional problems),

4

then he will be paid for the time and parts he has invested in the job.

An excellent example of this situation occurred at a shop that I was working in about 13 years ago. The other mechanic working with me was about 45 years old, had not taken any automotive classes (or had any other training) for at least 10 years, and was not ASE certified. He was just your basic, average mechanic--what's known in the industry as a "parts changer," not a highly-skilled technician. However, he had been working on cars for at least 20 years, and had a large following of loyal customers who trusted him and recommended him to all of their friends. (This story is also a good illustration of how worthless friends' recommendations can be.)

The car that he was working on had come in for "lack of power"--it wouldn't go over 35-40 miles per hour. Without doing any diagnostic tests, he told the customer that it probably just needed a good tune-up. When he was done tuning the engine, the problem was still there, so he told the customer that the carburetor also needed to be replaced.

This mechanic didn't know how to rebuild carburetors, so he always replaced them with new ones, which cost the customer about twice as much as rebuilding them. Since he didn't know enough about carburetors to rebuild them, he often misdiagnosed them as the cause of a problem.

After he replaced the carburetor, the problem was still there, so he told the customer that the timing chain and gears also needed to be replaced. The customer approved the additional repairs, so he installed the new chain and gears. When he was done, he said the car still didn't have any power, so I asked him if he had checked for a restricted exhaust system. He said he didn't think that was the problem, but I convinced him to disconnect the exhaust pipe and road test the car. With the pipe disconnected, the car ran great, so he sent it to a muffler shop to have the exhaust pipe replaced. (The inner wall of the pipe had collapsed, causing a restriction.)

This mechanic would definitely be considered incompetent, but he had not intended to deliberately sell that customer any unnecessary repairs--he was just trying to repair the car. I'm sure the customer was not told that the exhaust pipe was causing the problem, but he was charged for the tune-up, carburetor, and timing chain jobs that had nothing to do with the original complaint.

Unnecessary repairs occur every day in repair shops all over the country, but most of them are not a result of fraud--they are caused by mechanics who are incompetent because they haven't been properly educated and trained.

Why Are So Many Mechanics Incompetent?

Rapidly-changing technology is making most mechanics' skills obsolete. According to the California Bureau of Automotive Repair, which licenses mechanics for the state's smog inspection program, 70% of the mechanics being tested are not able to expertly diagnose and repair late-model vehicles.

The tests conducted by the Bureau cover basic diagnosis and repair of late-model (1980 or newer) emission control systems, carburetors, fuel injection, computer controls, and inspection procedures. Only 54% of the mechanics taking the test pass the first time (three attempts are permitted during a one-year period). Half of those who fail the first or second time reapply, but only 44-50% of them pass.

When I heard how few mechanics were passing the test, I decided to take it myself just to see how hard it really was. I only took the test once, and scored a 96%. (Minimum passing score was 79%.) Although it was a long test (150 questions), it was not that difficult. The material covered was not what I would consider advanced--all of the technical questions were on vehicle systems that have been around for 7-10 years.

After seeing how easy the state test was, the BAR figures would indicate that 50% of the mechanics don't even have a basic knowledge of vehicle technology that has been around for almost 10 years. I am in constant contact with many mechanics, and I think that is a fairly accurate assessment.

However, the state claims that 30% of the mechanics are able to expertly diagnose and repair late-model vehicles, and I have not found that to be true. Of all the mechanics (hundreds) that I talked to every month when I was involved in training, only a few seemed to be very knowledgeable concerning late-model vehicles. Several automotive instructors have also commented that they think less than 5% of all mechanics are able to expertly diagnose computer systems on late-model vehicles. (I agree.)

Why have so few mechanics kept up with the changes in technology? There are several reasons. Until about ten years ago, the best mechanics were usually the older ones with many years of experience, who were able to maintain their level of expertise without spending much (if any) time studying or going to school. Many of them chose that career because they didn't want to go to school, and they were able to do an adequate job without having to read. (Because of this, there were a lot of mechanics who couldn't read very well, but they are gradually being forced out of the industry.)

As vehicles became more complex, it was no longer possible to keep up with the latest technology without continuing education. Since many of the older mechanics had chosen that career because they had a strong dislike for reading or studying, they usually weren't willing to put in the effort that was necessary to upgrade their skills. Also, many older mechanics were "burned-out" on their trade and weren't interested in learning anything new. This is why many of the well-trained, highly-skilled technicians today are younger; they're willing to study and go to school because they're not "burned-out" yet.

To be fair, I must mention that an auto mechanic's job can be very stressful and exhausting. The last thing that most mechanics want to do after a long, hard day is go to a class from 6-10 P.M. I took a lot of night classes when I was working as a mechanic, and I would frequently fall asleep in class.

It's difficult to convince a lot of mechanics that they need additional training for two reasons--one is ignorance, and the other is a "macho" attitude that they already know everything so they don't need any training. I have talked to hundreds of mechanics who thought they understood late-model vehicles fairly well, until I started asking them questions. They obviously didn't know how to diagnose many problems without "guessing" (by installing new parts).

It seems that most mechanics would rather work on a vehicle for hours, replacing parts that they think are defective, before turning to a reference book for assistance. This tendency almost always results in unnecessary replacement of expensive electrical or computer components.

An article titled, "Auto Mechanics Struggle to Cope With Technology in Today's Cars" appeared in the *Wall Street Journal* on July 26, 1988. In the article, it was reported that approximately 40% of the engine-control computers returned as defective (by independent repair shops) to General Motors' Delco Electronics division were actually in perfect working order. According to the article, that figure has improved slightly since then, but not as much as Delco had hoped.

The *Journal* article shows how many "guesses" resulted in unnecessary repairs--40%. Since a typical bill for this type of repair is $200 (or more), consumers have been charged millions of dollars for repairs that weren't necessary. This is a common problem with repairs done on computer controls for two reasons--one, because most mechanics have not had enough training in this area, and two, because there isn't always a foolproof way to diagnose certain problems.

The last reason for the incompetence of many mechanics is their employers' unwillingness to provide or pay for continuing education. Some shop owners claim that they can't afford to pay for training, when they really can't afford not to; incompetent mechanics will cost them far more (in problems and lost profits) than the amount required to train them.

Some shop owners refuse to spend any money on upgrading their mechanics' skills because they're afraid their mechanics will quit after they're trained. (I guess they would rather have loyal, incompetent mechanics than pay enough to keep well-trained, highly-skilled ones.) This is an extremely short-sighted and unwise way to run an auto repair business.

Honest Mistakes--Who Pays for Them?

I don't believe it's possible to completely eliminate unnecessary repairs, but it is possible to drastically reduce how often it happens to you by choosing a mechanic who is educated and certified. (Be sure to read the chapter titled, "Finding Mechanics You Can Trust" for more information.) A mechanic who is able to pass the ASE certification tests, and continues to attend classes to keep up with

9

the latest changes in automotive technology, is less likely to make a lot of mistakes that you will end up paying for.

I am not happy with the practice of charging customers for unnecessary repairs when the mechanic makes an incorrect diagnosis, because it costs consumers millions of dollars every year, but most shops would go broke if they had to give away parts and labor every time they made a mistake. If mechanics could tell their customers the truth without getting in a lot of hot water, it would make it a lot easier for consumers to tell whether they have a good mechanic or not.

For those of you who are outraged at this happening at all (especially to you), consider the fact that doctors do the same thing all the time. When is the last time you heard a doctor say that he made a mistake and was willing to either treat you for free or give you your money back? What usually happens is that your doctor will say something like, "Since that didn't seem to work, we are going to try something else." Of course, you get to pay for everything he tries until he guesses correctly.

Today's vehicles have become so complex that a mechanic is sometimes forced to make an educated guess, in the same way that doctors have to guess, because there isn't always a foolproof way to diagnose a particular problem. However, the customer has a right to know that the mechanic is making an educated guess and that his vehicle may still need additional repairs before it is operating properly.

When I was working as a mechanic, I sometimes had to make educated guesses. I found that by informing the customer that there was no foolproof diagnosis for that problem and that it was necessary to make an educated guess, if it turned out that my guess was wrong, they were not upset with me and I did not have to lie to get paid for the work I had done. Encourage your mechanic to do the same and you will soon find out how often he is guessing, and also how "educated" his guesses really are.

Sometimes a mechanic will accidentally break a part or otherwise damage a vehicle that he is working on. How this type of problem is resolved indicates how honest a shop really is--an honest one will pay for whatever is broken.

The last shop that I worked in, an independent, AAA-approved shop with four mechanics, was the most honest shop I had ever worked in as a mechanic. Occasionally one of us would accidentally break something and the shop owner would repair or replace whatever was damaged free of charge to the customer.

A situation that seems to be far more common (based on my experience) occurred in another shop that I worked in briefly. A customer had brought his car in for some routine work--a lube and oil change, tune-up, valve adjustment, etc. The car ran fine, but it had been a long time since it was last serviced.

While one of the mechanics was changing the spark plugs, he dropped a small screw over the engine. After searching awhile, he gave up and finished installing the plugs. When he attempted to start the engine, it only turned over briefly before locking up.

The "missing screw" had gone into one of the spark plug holes and was now lodged between the piston and valve. The mechanic could see the screw through the spark plug hole, but it was too deeply imbedded in the piston to remove through the hole. He finally succeeded in getting the engine to crank over, but it was now running very rough because the valve had been damaged.

It was now obvious to everyone in the shop that the mechanic had seriously damaged the engine. When he told the shop owner what had happened, the owner was initially upset, but then he said, "Don't worry, I'll just tell

11

the customer that we discovered some more problems when we were adjusting the valves and that it needs a valve job to prevent serious engine damage." The customer bought the story "hook, line, and sinker" and ended up paying the shop about $800 to repair the damage caused by the mechanic.

This customer could have avoided paying for this unnecessary repair if he would have been a little more suspicious of the need for such a major repair when his car ran so well before he brought it to the shop. He should have told them that he didn't want the additional work done that day, and taken his car to another shop for a second opinion; then he would have had enough evidence to make the first shop repair his car for free (or pay for him to get it repaired at another shop).

I only worked at this shop for about two months. After witnessing the above incident and several more like it, I started looking for another job in a shop where the management and employees had a little more integrity.

COMMISSION SHOPS

Instead of paying their mechanics the prevailing wage based on their skill levels and experience, many auto repair shops pay them a base salary plus a commission on the dollar volume of additional repair work that they sell. Because this practice encourages the sale of unnecessary repairs, it is fraught with abuse. A basic knowledge of how this practice works, as well as the types of shops that use it, can help you to avoid becoming a victim.

In an area where the typical salary range for a decent (but not exceptional) mechanic would be about $550-600 per week, a mechanic in a typical commission shop would be paid a base salary of about $300-350 per week, plus a commission of 10-25% on all additional repair work that he sells. For a mechanic working in a commission shop to end up making enough money to live on, he will have to earn about $250-300 per week in commissions.

What this means to the customers of that shop is that the mechanic has to sell between $200 and $400 in additional repairs *every day* just to make a decent living. For example, a mechanic in a typical tune-up shop will tune 5-6 cars per day, so he needs to sell an average of $50 in additional repair work to every customer.

However, not all customers will buy additional repairs, so the mechanic needs to get even more money from the ones who are willing and able. If he manages to convince two-thirds of his customers to buy additional repairs, he will have to get an extra $70-100 from each of them.

Abuses occur when the mechanic runs across too many vehicles that really need additional repairs, but the owners can't afford to have the work done. (This is a fairly common situation--vehicles that need a lot of work are usually in that condition because the owners don't have the money to get them fixed.) Now the mechanic is in a real predicament, because he is forced to choose between not making enough money to pay his bills and selling unnecessary repairs to the remaining customers. For a mechanic with a family to support, the temptation is often too great.

Repair shops that use the salary-plus-commission arrangement described above usually advertise heavily, offering low-priced service specials and even free inspections. Typical ads might read, "Tune-up $39.95," "Brake Reline $59.95," "Transmission Service $29.95," "Free Brake Inspections," etc. (See the chapters covering specific repairs for more details on how specials like these have been used to attract many unsuspecting customers, who were then sold unnecessary repairs.)

The only reason that repair shops offer specials is to bring in a lot of new customers so they can sell them additional repairs; most shops would go broke if the only work they did was at the special prices.

To be on the safe side, try to find an educated, ASE-certified mechanic who is not paid a commission on sales; that way he won't have any incentive to sell you unnecessary repairs. If you're not sure how a shop's mechanics are paid, ask the shop owner or mechanics. Most of them are willing to provide this information (often over the phone) if they have nothing to hide, so if you can't get a straight answer, find another shop.

NOTE--

Not all low-priced or commission shops intentionally sell unnecessary repairs. This section was written to inform the public of how the payment of sales commissions to mechanics has resulted in abuses in the past. Consumers *can* save money by using advertised specials, as long as the work is done by qualified professionals, no unnecessary repairs are made, and quality parts are used. Unfortunately, this is often not the case.

Also, some shops pay their mechanics a "commission" based on completed repairs, a practice also known as "flat rate" payment, which usually doesn't encourage the sale of unnecessary repairs. For example, a mechanic may receive 40% of the labor charges instead of an hourly wage.

The advantage of this practice for consumers is that it tends to keep labor costs down because the mechanic is only paid for the amount of time the job is supposed to take. The disadvantage is that sometimes a mechanic is encouraged to get the job done as fast as possible so he makes more money, sometimes resulting in poor workmanship.

CHAPTER 2

Brake Shops

Note: This chapter deals mainly with shops that specialize in brake work and advertise low-priced brake relines.
Some of these shops may also specialize in other repairs,
which may be reflected in their name--for example, "ABC
Tune & Brake" or "XYZ Muffler & Brake." The material
in this chapter may also apply to general repair shops if
they use the same advertising, pricing, or sales tactics as
those outlined here.

You've probably seen ads for $59 or $69 brake relines, re-
alizing that most shops charge twice that amount. Why
do you think those shops charge so much less? Because
they're "nice guys" and the other shops are just greedy?
Or is there a catch?

There is a catch. First, the $120 brake reline usually
includes rebuilding the wheel cylinders; the $59 brake job
does not. Second, very few people actually get their
brakes done for only $59; most people are sold additional
parts and repairs, increasing the final bill much higher
than $120. (A 1993 investigation by the New York Attor-
ney General into practices at Midas Muffler and Brake
Shops found that 88% of the people who went there for
$59-69 brake jobs ending up paying over three-and-a-half

times the advertised price.)

It's pretty hard for a shop to make a decent profit on a $59 or $69 brake reline, so why do they advertise them? So they can sell a lot of (usually high-priced) additional repairs to the people who come in for the specials. It's not uncommon for a customer to receive a revised estimate for $300-400 after bringing a vehicle in for a $59 brake reline.

When a shop consistently tells people that their vehicles need more repairs than the special includes, and then tries to sell them the additional repairs that they supposedly need, that shop is guilty of illegal "bait and switch" sales tactics.

How do these shops convince so many people that they need $300-400 brake jobs, especially after they came in for the $59 special? Scare tactics.

Brake shops probably have more potential for consumer fraud than any other type of repair shop. For most drivers, a vehicle that runs rough or makes noise is irritating, but a vehicle without brakes is absolutely frightening. Many unethical shops have taken advantage of this fear, using scare tactics to sell unnecessary (and usually high-priced) brake repairs.

Shops that use dishonest "bait and switch" tactics know that there are plenty of people who will go to an unfamiliar shop for repairs if they think that shop has the lowest prices in town. They also know that there are plenty of people who think they can get something for nothing (like a "free" inspection).

How does a dishonest shop find enough customers to stay in business and make piles of money? All they have to do is offer free brake inspections or cheap brake relines, and they will have what seems to be an endless supply of victims.

In the past, many of these shops advertised free brake

inspections, but the public must have figured out that it was just a scheme to sell brake repairs, so now they offer "free safety inspections" instead. This also gives shops an opportunity to sell other (sometimes unnecessary) repair work.

Most shops that advertise low-priced brake relines or free inspections pay their mechanics a commission on sales in addition to a small salary. The salary is usually only 40-50% of the going rate for a good mechanic, so their mechanics have to sell a lot of additional repairs just to earn a living.

This practice of paying mechanics a sales commission (instead of a decent wage) encourages the sale of unnecessary repairs, especially when business is slow or there is a lack of willing customers who really need additional repairs. If business slows down for a while, a mechanic who doesn't sell unnecessary repairs may not make enough money to live on.

The large amount of unnecessary repairs that have been sold would seem to indicate that most of the mechanics working in those shops are dishonest. I don't believe that's true. What I do believe is at least partially responsible for the large-scale abuses (especially at the well-known chains) is the lack of knowledge and proper training on the part of the mechanics combined with greed (and dishonesty, in some cases) on the part of the shop owners and managers.

Most of the mechanics who go to work for the low-priced brake shops are not well-trained, highly-skilled technicians. They're what's known in the industry as "parts changers," which is a name given to less-skilled mechanics who replace a lot of parts, instead of diagnosing and repairing only the defective item(s).

This explains why they are willing to work for a low salary plus commission. If they were highly-skilled, they could easily get a job somewhere else at a considerably higher salary, without having to sell any additional repairs.

Since their mechanics are usually not well-trained, it's easier to convince them that they're doing the customer a favor by replacing a lot of parts that don't appear to be defective. They are often told by management that certain parts should be replaced to prevent future problems. Training programs put on by the company, and by parts suppliers, are usually geared toward selling more parts.

The following true stories are excellent examples of how these shops use free inspections and low-priced brake relines to attract a lot of people, and then try to sell them high-priced repairs.

A casual acquaintance of mine had his brakes inspected at another shop, where he was told that he needed a front brake reline. They said it would cost about $125 for parts and labor. Trying to save some money, he decided to get several estimates before having the work done. When he asked me for an estimate, I told him it would cost about $120. He said he would think it over and call me back.

I saw him a week later, and asked what he had decided to do with his brakes. He told me that he had taken his car to a well-known brake shop that was advertising a brake reline for $59. After he left his car with them, they called and told him that his brakes were in bad shape, and that additional repairs were necessary. They told him it would cost about $500 to "do the brakes properly." Unfortunately for him, he told them to go ahead and do the work. (He asked if I thought he had been ripped-off, and I said that he probably was.)

Another time, I received a phone call at the shop from one of our customers. She had taken her car to a shop for their advertised "free brake inspection." (This shop was part of the same well-known brake chain that sold the other person a $500 brake job.) They told her that her brakes were in pretty bad shape and that it would cost about $500 to repair them.

She had called to ask if I thought that was too much money to pay for a brake job. I told her that price was pretty high, and that if her brakes really were in such bad shape, someone would have noticed. So I pulled the repair orders on her car from our files to see if any recommendations had been made for brake repairs.

We had done a routine service about two months prior to that and had inspected her brakes at that time. The notes on the repair order stated that the brakes were in good shape, with about 80% of the brake lining remaining (her brakes should have gone at least another 20-25,000 miles). The drums, calipers, and wheel cylinders were all in good condition when we inspected them.

When I read the notes to her, she said she didn't understand why they were telling her that her brakes were so bad when we had just said they were all right. My response was that it looked like they were trying to sell her repairs that weren't needed and that she should not allow them to do any work on her car. I also recommended that she file a complaint against that shop with the Bureau of Automotive Repair.

These were not isolated incidents--I have heard similar stories from many people concerning brake shops belonging to the same chain.

Undercover Investigations, 1986-89
Midas Muffler & Brake Shops, California

After receiving numerous consumer complaints, the California Bureau of Automotive Repair and district attorney's offices from four counties started an undercover investigation of ten Midas Muffler & Brake Shops. The shops were all individually-owned franchises, and were located in four counties.

A 15-month investigation, ending in 1986, resulted in nine of the Midas shops being charged in civil complaints with fraudulent business practices. The charges included making "false and misleading statements in order to sell automotive services, parts, and repairs," charging customers more than the estimated price, performing repairs "in an incompetent manner," and recommending repairs that were not needed.

The shops were also charged with offering free safety checks to get people to bring in their cars, then after the cars were up on a hoist and inoperative, mechanics would say that repairs were needed, even if they weren't.

Undercover vehicles with practically all new brake parts were taken to the shops. (For example, some vehicles had worn-out brake shoes, but all other brake parts were new.) According to the Bureau, investigators posing as customers documented the sale of unnecessary repairs; some of the brake parts that were replaced were brand-new, with less than 50 miles on them.

A deputy district attorney who worked on the case claimed that the Midas shops used scare tactics that were designed to close the sale, leading customers to believe that brake failure was so imminent that they shouldn't drive their car to another shop for a lower price or a second opinion. In what he claimed was an example of practices at the shops, a woman who had taken her car to one of the shops for brake work was given a worksheet that said her brake master cylinder was "ready to blow."

The Midas shops were also charged with routinely selling new coil springs that were not needed. One of the deputy district attorneys stated that the shops tried to sell new springs to practically all consumers who brought in certain General Motors vehicles. (Similar charges were made against a large Midas shop in Michigan.)

To settle the case out of court, Midas International agreed to pay a civil judgment of $100,000 and the individual shops agreed to pay an additional $400,000. (This settlement also involved muffler advertising and repairs. See the chapter titled, "Muffler Shops" for more details.) A permanent injunction was entered against all Midas Muffler & Brake Shops in California, prohibiting the sale of unnecessary parts and repairs.

In 1989, undercover investigations of six more Midas shops in California resulted in charges of fraudulent business practices for allegedly recommending and/or selling unnecessary repairs, in violation of the court order. Most of the shops were put on probation for three years.

Undercover Investigation--Pennsylvania, 1989
Midas Muffler & Brake Shops,
Goodyear Auto Service Center,
Avellino's Tire & Auto Service Center

The state Bureau of Consumer Protection had received numerous complaints of the alleged sale of unnecessary brake repairs, so an undercover investigation was set up to go "shopping" at 35 auto repair centers in southeastern Pennsylvania. The Bureau shopped not only at repair centers that had generated numerous complaints, but at others as well.

Undercover cars were prepared by the Keystone AAA Diagnostic Center so the brakes were in good working condition; some vehicles had new brakes. Minor problems were then created immediately before the vehicles were taken to the repair shops.

In some cases, wear indicators on new disc brake pads were intentionally bent, causing the brakes to squeal. Investigators claim that they were sold new disc pads to cure the problem, when all that was needed was to bend the wear indicators so they didn't touch the rotors. In other cases, air was pumped into a brake line, causing a low brake pedal. Investigators said they were sold new master cylinders, when all that was needed to cure the problem was to bleed the air out of the system.

As a result of the investigation, four Midas Muffler & Brake Shops, two Avellino's Tire & Auto Service Centers, and one Goodyear Tire Center were accused of recommending or performing unnecessary brake repairs. The Bureau claimed that each shop tried to sell unnecessary repairs on two or three occasions. One of the Midas shops was owned by the parent company, Midas International; the other three were franchises. The Goodyear store was also owned by its parent company, Goodyear Tire & Rubber Co.

To settle the charges, the operators of the four Midas shops agreed to pay total civil penalties of $7,000; the operator of Avellino's $2,700; and Goodyear $2,500. They also promised not to violate state law or to "knowingly misrepresent that services, replacements, or repairs are needed if they are not needed."

Undercover Investigations, 1991-92
Midas Muffler & Brake Shops, Pennsylvania

Charges of deceptive business practices were filed by the Attorney General against 12 Midas Muffler & Brake Shops in the Pittsburgh area following an undercover investigation. In a joint operation between the city police, state police, and the state Bureau of Consumer Protection, a female detective posing as a consumer visited 10 Midas shops selected at random from the phone book.

Driving a car that was previously inspected under the

supervision of the State Police, the detective went to the shops and requested a state inspection or safety check. Three of the shops were charged with issuing inspection certificates after failing to detect repairs needed to bring the vehicle into compliance with state inspection requirements.

All of the shops visited were charged with failing to note serious safety defects, and some with recommending unnecessary repairs. In addition to the 10 shops, two others were charged with recommending hundreds of dollars worth of unnecessary brake repairs after consumer complaints were filed with the state.

The 12 Midas franchises settled the case after agreeing to pay the state $51,250 for the costs of the investigation and to resolve the consumer complaints by providing refunds or additional repairs at no charge. They also promised to "work in good faith" with the state to settle any outstanding complaints.

In an unrelated 1992 Philadelphia investigation, four company-owned Midas shops were visited by state undercover cars. One of the shops was charged with recommending $452 in unnecessary repairs; the other three did not recommend any repairs that weren't needed. To settle the charges, Midas agreed to pay $10,000 in penalties and costs of the investigation.

That same year in Michigan, one Midas shop was charged with falsely representing that repairs were needed, charging for repairs that were not done, and other lesser violations. The shop paid a $1,000 penalty and was put on probation for 24 months.

BRAKE GUIDELINES

A brake reline should include the following: thorough inspection of brake system; new, high-quality brake lining;

resurface rotors or drums; rebuild wheel cylinders; repack wheel bearings and install new grease seals (except for sealed bearings on front wheel drive vehicles); bleed and adjust brakes; road test to verify proper operation.

On vehicles with drum brakes, the wheel cylinders should be rebuilt when new brake shoes are installed, usually every 40-50,000 miles. If this is not done, there is a good chance that the cylinders will start leaking (or even blow out) long before the brake lining wears out.

Some shops refuse to rebuild wheel cylinders. They claim that rebuilt ones are not as reliable as new ones and that it takes too much time to rebuild them, so the customer doesn't save any money. I don't agree with either statement--I've rebuilt many wheel cylinders over the last 20 years and had just as many problems with new ones as the ones I rebuilt.

The secret lies in knowing which ones can be rebuilt and which ones should be replaced. Cast iron wheel cylinders can usually be rebuilt, unless the bores are pitted, but it's probably a good idea to just replace the aluminum ones. Mechanics who have had too many problems with cylinders they've rebuilt obviously rebuilt ones that should have been thrown out with the trash.

As far as cost is concerned, it only takes 2 or 3 more minutes to rebuild a wheel cylinder than it does to replace one, so the customer can save $40-50 (per axle) on a brake job if they're not replaced. So why do so many shops insist on replacing them? Because they make more money--in less time--by selling new ones.

On most vehicles, especially late-models, the disc brake calipers don't need to be rebuilt or replaced every time new disc pads are installed. Because their design is totally different from that of wheel cylinders, many calipers last well over 100,000 miles without requiring any repairs (except for certain Chrysler products). They should only be repaired or replaced if obvious defects exist (for example, stuck pistons, fluid leaks, damaged dust seals, etc.).

It's not necessary to rebuild or replace the master cylinder every time the brakes are relined; on many vehicles, the original master cylinder will last well over 100,000 miles. Replacement is only necessary if there are signs of external or internal leaks. (An internal leak will cause the brake pedal to "sink" towards the floor when pressure is applied. This is especially noticeable when the vehicle is stopped.)

High-quality, rebuilt calipers and wheel cylinders are all right, but I do not recommend installing rebuilt master cylinders. I have seen too many of them fail, and I don't think it's worth risking total brake failure just to save $40-50.

Rotors and drums should be resurfaced when new brake pads or shoes are installed. Rotor or drum replacement is not usually necessary, unless the vehicle was driven for a while after the brake lining wore out and there was metal-to-metal contact. They should only be replaced if they are below the factory-recommended minimum thickness after resurfacing, as measured with a micrometer. Make sure they are measured--don't settle for someone's "expert opinion" or "experience."

Don't let someone sell you new rotors or drums just because every little line won't come out when they are resurfaced. As long as at least 95% of the surface is smooth, small lines will not affect the life or operation of the brakes.

Some brake shops try to sell hardware kits (springs, clips, etc.) on every brake job they do, but most of this is unnecessary. Brake hardware only needs to be replaced if it's damaged, not just because it's "old." For example, a drum brake return spring that has a gap between the coils has been damaged by excessive heat and should be replaced.

Brake lining, wheel cylinders, and return springs should only be replaced in axle sets (for example, if new return springs are installed on one of the rear brakes, make sure the other rear brake also gets new springs). Failure to do this may result in erratic and/or unsafe braking.

A common scam used by brake shops involves telling customers that all four brakes should be relined, even though only the fronts (or the rears) are bad. Don't fall for this! It's not necessary to reline all of the brakes just because those on one axle need to be done. Unless there are obvious defects in the brake lining (for example, heat cracks or large chips), the lining doesn't usually need replacement until it is worn down to 25-30% of the original thickness.

Beware of shops that tell you that it's necessary to do a complete brake reline to cure a brake squeak. Although a metal-to-metal grinding noise in the brakes indicates a serious (and often expensive) problem, a brake squeak does not necessarily mean that anything is wrong.

Replacing the brake lining and turning the rotors (or drums) will get rid of a brake squeak, but the noise often returns within several months. What causes this squeak? Any of the following conditions: brake lining that's glazed from excessive heat; excessive brake dust in a drum brake; contamination of the brake lining from mud puddles, antifreeze, oil, or grease; or disc pads vibrating in the calipers.

If the brake lining got so hot that it has heat cracks, or if it was contaminated by antifreeze, oil, or grease, then the lining should be replaced. The other listed conditions do not warrant lining replacement because they won't affect the vehicle's stopping ability; also, those conditions can reoccur quickly even after new lining is installed.

Instead of just selling a customer a brake job to cure a brake squeak, a competent and honest mechanic will explain to him that there may not be anything wrong with the brakes, and even if the brakes were relined to stop the noise, it could come back anyway within several months.

A WORD OF ADVICE

When your vehicle needs brake work, find a reputable, highly-skilled mechanic. His estimate may seem higher than some shops because he uses higher quality parts than they do. It also may seem higher because he's giving you an honest estimate, with no hidden surprises, and the other shops aren't. Shopping around for the lowest price will only increase your chances of being ripped off. Insist on the use of high-quality parts; brakes are too important to try saving a few dollars by using cheap parts.

CHAPTER 3

Tire & Alignment Shops

Many tire & alignment shops pay their employees a sales commission (or bonus) for parts and services that are sold to the customer. Training sessions, "pep talks," contests, and prizes for the most sales are often used to motivate employees to sell as much as possible, a practice that encourages the sale of unnecessary parts and services.

If a vehicle is brought in for new tires, the salesman or workers will often try to sell the customer an alignment, new valve stems, front end parts, shock absorbers, and/or strut cartridges. Mechanics doing front end alignments will often try to sell major front end repairs like ball joints, idler arms, tie rod ends, control arm bushings, etc. (If your vehicle is ten years old, it may very well need some of these items, but if it's only three or four years old, it probably doesn't.) Dishonest sales tactics, some of which are described in the sections below, are often used to convince the customer that those parts need to be replaced.

Unscrupulous mechanics and salesmen sometimes use scare tactics to sell additional parts and repairs, especially with female customers. They might say that a wheel could fall off or the steering could go out if certain parts aren't replaced. *Don't fall for this trick!* It is extremely rare for a wheel to fall off, or steering to go out, without any warning.

A front end part that is bad enough to cause total steering loss will usually have other symptoms for weeks (or months) before it finally breaks. A vibration or shimmy in the front end; sloppy or erratic steering; or squeaking, grinding, or clunking noises should be checked as soon as possible to make sure the vehicle is safe to drive.

Beware of advertisements for low-priced front end alignments!! Generally speaking, these shops are not trying to make more money just by doing more alignments. In fact, they would probably *lose* money if low-priced alignments were the only repairs they did. These ads are designed to bring in more customers so the shop can sell them additional high-profit repairs.

The auto repair business is so labor-intensive, and so much expensive equipment is required to operate a shop, that it's virtually impossible to make money by offering lower prices without "cutting corners" somewhere. Some of the "corners" that are cut include hiring lower-paid (i.e. less-skilled) workers, not doing a thorough (high-quality) job, and/or charging high-quality prices for low-quality parts.

An excellent example of how some of these shops cut corners on low-priced alignments is a common practice known as "set the toe and let it go." Instead of checking and adjusting the caster, camber, and toe settings (which are all part of a complete alignment), the mechanic will only adjust the toe setting. By skipping the other two adjustments, he can complete the job in 10-15 minutes, instead of the 40-50 minutes (or more) that it normally takes to do an alignment properly.

Another practice that has been around for a long time consists of the mechanic using a pair of pliers to scratch the nuts and bolts on the tie rod sleeves to make it look like adjustments were made, when they weren't. The mechanic may or may not even hook up the alignment equipment to the vehicle, depending on whether he thinks someone is watching or not. This practice is definitely fraudulent because the customer is charged for an alignment even though no adjustments were made.

I have seen both of these practices used many times, especially when a low-priced alignment is being done after the shop failed to sell the customer additional repairs. So, be prepared for a sales pitch designed to sell you additional repairs if you take your vehicle to a shop that is advertising an unusually low-priced alignment (30-50% lower than the normal prices charged by most shops in the area).

If your vehicle is in one of these shops to have the tires replaced and the front end aligned, and you are told that they can't do the alignment unless they replace some of the front end parts, tell them to forget the alignment and front end work for now because you hadn't planned on spending that much money.

Tell them that you need to think it over and you will get back to them in a day or two, then take your vehicle to another shop for a second opinion. (Don't tell the first shop what you plan to do, as it may affect how they treat you in the future if they are irritated or offended.)

At this point, they may tell you that the new tires will be ruined if you drive on them without repairing the front end first. They might even tell you that the warranty on the tires will be void if you don't have the work done immediately. *Don't fall for this!* The new tires will only be ruined if the front end is in really bad shape and you drive on the new tires for a lot longer than several days before the repairs are done. Besides, if the front end really was that bad, you probably would have noticed a front end shimmy, a pull to one side, or erratic steering; also, your old tires would have shown signs of uneven and rapid wear.

The warranty on new tires can only be voided if misalignment or worn parts cause uneven tire wear, which is not going to happen in a couple of days. Also, (by law) they can't require that all necessary repairs be done at their shop to keep the warranty in force--you can do them yourself or have them done at another shop.

To get a second opinion, take your vehicle to a regular repair shop that does alignments, preferably one that employs ASE certified mechanics and does not pay its employees a sales commission. Ask them to check the front end, but don't tell them about the first diagnosis until you get theirs. (Expect to pay for at least 15-20 minutes of labor for this). If they don't find any bad front end parts, or if they don't recommend replacing as many parts as the first shop did, have them do the repairs and the alignment instead of the shop with the alignment "special."

Their charge for the alignment may be higher than the first shop, but remember--the second shop didn't try to sell you as many additional parts; besides, the first shop wouldn't do the alignment at the lower price without first doing all of the repairs that they recommended. (If the second shop recommends fewer repairs, or none at all, you get an additional bonus--now you know where to go for honest front end work.)

When I was working in an independent repair shop, we had quite a few customers who came to us for a second opinion after some tire & alignment shops (with low-priced alignment specials) told them that their vehicles needed front end work before an alignment could be done. (Most of those shops were well-known nationwide tire centers or department store automotive centers.) In most cases, we found that the recommended repairs were unnecessary and we were able to align the vehicles without replacing any parts.

Some shops try to sell alignments to practically everyone who brings their vehicle in, especially if they're buying new tires. If the old tires had uneven wear (for example, if a tire was only "bald" on one side), then the alignment should definitely be checked and adjusted if necessary. However, if the old tires wore evenly and lasted quite a while (40-50,000 miles), then it would probably be a waste of money to have the front end aligned.

If any major front end work is done (for example, ball joints, tie rods, tie rod ends, idler arms, drag links, control arms, springs, or a rack and pinion assembly), the alignment should be checked because replacing these parts can cause it to change. Replacing the tires or the shocks doesn't change the alignment, so don't let someone sell you an unnecessary alignment just because these items are replaced.

A common practice that I think is a scam is that of charging the full alignment price when the alignment is checked and no adjustments are necessary. Usually, when this happens, the customer doesn't realize that no adjustments were made because he's told that the alignment was off and they adjusted it.

If a shop is dishonest, there probably isn't much you can do once they have your vehicle, which is why it's so important to check them out before you take your vehicle to their shop. One thing you can do is ask them what their policy is when they check an alignment and discover that no adjustments are necessary. If they don't reply quickly with an answer such as, "When that happens, we only charge X dollars for checking it, instead of the full price," it's fairly safe to assume that they charge everyone the full alignment price, whether it was necessary or not.

The charge for checking an alignment should be 1/3 to 1/2 of the normal alignment price. Also ask them how often that happens. A shop that only does one alignment per day should run across at least one car a month that didn't need any adjustments; a shop that does 5-10 alignments per day should see that more often.

Before taking your vehicle to a tire/alignment shop, call the shop and ask how their workers are paid--hourly, salary, or commission. If they won't tell you, find another shop. If they say their workers are paid a commission, ask whether it's based on sales or a percentage of labor (which is known as "flat rate") instead of an hourly wage.

Since workers who are paid an hourly wage, salary, or flat rate have no incentive to sell additional parts and services, a shop that uses any of these pay scales for its workers is less likely to sell unnecessary repairs than one that pays its workers a sales commission.

Sometimes a commission shop can save you money on advertised specials, if you don't allow them to sell you anything else. However, since these shops usually don't make any money on a special unless they sell additional work, it is very likely that you will be pressured to buy something else. If you decide to use a commission shop anyway, be sure to get a second opinion before having any major work done; don't give immediate approval for any major repairs that you didn't initially request.

"LIFETIME ALIGNMENTS"

Some tire and alignment shops sell "lifetime alignments," which supposedly allow the customer to pay only once, thereafter receiving "free" alignments for as long as he owns that vehicle. Since the usual price for this service is slightly less than the normal charge for two alignments, it would appear to be a good deal for the customer.

What's wrong with this "good deal"? Think about it. Why would a shop offer to do three, four, or more alignments on a vehicle when they only got paid for two? The answer is simple--at most, they might do one free alignment; in many cases they won't have to do any at all. How can they get away with this? Simple--statistics and fine print.

First, many customers will either forget that they paid for a lifetime alignment or they will sell the vehicle before they (attempt to) get a free alignment. Second, the fine print of the warranty says that it may be necessary to replace some parts before an alignment can be done. Of course, an additional charge for parts and labor will be made if this is necessary.

So, instead of giving away free alignments, all they have to do is tell customers that their vehicles can't be aligned until some of the parts are replaced. Most people won't want to throw away the money they "invested" in the lifetime alignment, so they approve the additional repairs, becoming victims of unnecessary repair schemes. The lifetime alignment becomes a psychological hook to tie a customer to the repair shop.

Because this practice encourages the sale of unnecessary repairs, I do not recommend that consumers purchase this service.

If you have already purchased a lifetime alignment and would like to get your money's worth, take your vehicle back to the shop for free alignments, but don't authorize any additional repairs without going to another shop for a second opinion (and a second estimate).

You can also have any necessary repairs done elsewhere, so shop around. By law, a shop can't require you to have any repairs done there to maintain a warranty. If you refuse to buy anything else, don't be surprised if the shop personnel become irritated and start making excuses about why they can't align your vehicle. After all, they never intended to give out free alignments without selling additional repairs.

Undercover Investigations, 1992-93
Winston Tire Company, California

After conducting a lengthy undercover investigation of 37 Winston Tire stores throughout the state, the California Bureau of Automotive Repair charged the company with selling unnecessary repairs and billing for parts that were not installed. The Bureau said that in 74% of the undercover runs, the stores tried to sell unnecessary parts and repairs, or bill for parts that weren't installed. According to one of the deputy district attorneys working on the case, overcharges on the undercover cars averaged $189 for shocks, springs, and brake parts.

When the Sears investigation made headlines in 1992, Winston management voluntarily made changes in its sales practices to ensure that the none of their stores were selling unnecessary repairs. (Both companies had been using sales commissions, contests, and other sales incentives.) However, it was too late--they were already under investigation.

To settle the charges, Winston agreed to pay $1.4 million, which included penalties, costs of investigation, and $450,000 in restitution to consumers. The state said Winston cooperated fully, without fighting the charges, and even went beyond the requirements of the settlement in putting safeguards into place to make sure no more problems occur. (See Chapter 19 for details of the new safeguards.)

Winston Tire had previously been charged with selling unnecessary repairs in Ventura County after a 1988 undercover investigation that involved shocks and front end parts. Winston agreed to pay $100,000 in civil penalties, costs, and restitution to settle the charges.

Undercover Investigations, 1992-93
Big O Tire, California

The owners of an 18-store chain of Big O Tire shops in Orange County were charged by the Bureau with fraudulent business practices following an undercover investigation into 5 of their stores. (Charges were only made against CSB Partnership, the owners of the 18 stores, not against the parent company or any other franchisees.)

After receiving a number of consumer complaints for the five stores, undercover cars were sent to the shops, where they detected a pattern of selling unnecessary repairs including brake hardware, rear coil springs, shocks, master cylinders, and disc brake calipers. The average oversell was $397.

To settle the charges of fraudulent or misleading statements and advertising, and exceeding repair estimates without authorization, the owners agreed to pay $169,000 in penalties, costs of investigation, and restitution.

As a result of other unrelated undercover investigations in 1993-94, three Big O Tire franchises in Northern California were also charged with the sale of unnecessary repairs.

Undercover Investigation, 1989
Goodyear Auto Centers,
Firestone Service Center,
Belle Tire Center, Michigan

Channel 2 TV (WJBK) was planning a show for consumers on auto repair and they wanted to film some repair shops trying to sell unnecessary repairs, so they asked the Michigan Bureau of Auto Regulation which shops they should visit. They were told to go to the ones that advertised heavily in the local newspapers for low-priced alignments and brake jobs, or free inspections.

The station had a two-year old car thoroughly checked by automotive experts at the Bureau and the engineering firm of ECS/Roush, who verified that the front end and brake systems did not need any repairs. Male and female reporters were fitted with hidden microphones, then they took the car on a "shopping" trip to twelve repair centers in the Detroit area for an alignment or brake inspection.

It's interesting to note here that the target shops were chosen solely on the basis of their ads for low-priced repairs and/or free inspections. They were not chosen based on consumer complaints.

Channel 2 reporters said that four of the shops misrepresented the need for repairs by telling the reporters that the vehicle needed new struts or brakes. Two of the shops were Goodyear Auto Centers (one of which was company-owned), one was a Firestone Service Center, and the other was a Belle Tire Center.

According to Channel 2, employees at both Goodyear stores told the reporters that the car needed new struts (MacPherson strut cartridges). At one of the stores, the reporter was told, "You got one strut here that's beating the snubber on the ground, too. It's been coming down and beating the snubber right out of it. Boom! Boom! You getting any noise out of it?" However, the camera showed that the snubbers were still in excellent condition; you could even read the GM logos and part numbers that were on them. Reporters claimed the Goodyear store also said the tires needed to be replaced, but the Bureau expert who checked the tires said he saw no reason to replace them.

At the Belle Tire store, the reporter was told the alignment couldn't be done because the struts were bad. The following conversation was recorded with the hidden microphone: [mechanic] "We recommend that, since they're going bad now, not to align it." [reporter] "You didn't align it?" [mechanic] "No--it won't hold an alignment." (What makes this statement outrageous is that even if the struts were bad, it still wouldn't be true.)

A Channel 2 reporter went back to the shops (with a camera and microphone) and confronted them with the allegation that they had tried to sell repairs that weren't needed, but the shops defended their diagnosis. The tapes were aired in the station's five-part series on auto repair, which included a message from the Bureau on how consumers can avoid rip-offs.

In defense of their diagnosis, one of the shops allegedly claimed that Oldsmobile recommends strut replacement at 45,000 miles. (The car used was an Olds with 43,000 miles.) A General Motors spokesman called the station to say that wasn't true--GM has no mileage replacement recommendation on struts. The company's philosophy is that they should only be replaced when they're worn out.

In 1974, Channel 2 did a similar investigation of 25 repair shops which indicated that 1/3 of the shops were dishonest, and 1/3 were incompetent. This investigation was instrumental in getting the state legislature to pass a tough auto repair law.

Unrelated investigations have resulted in charges of selling unauthorized repairs at other Firestone stores:
1993--Visalia, CA, $120,000 settlement, 1 store.
1992--West Bloomfield, MI, $1,150 penalty, 1 store.
1984--Ventura County, CA, $150,000 settlement.

Undercover Investigation, 1992-93
Goodyear Auto Centers, Minnesota

Starting in October of 1992, KSTP-TV (Channel 2) sent undercover cars to 7 company-owned Goodyear Auto

Centers in the Saint Paul area. A three month investigation was done using hidden cameras and specially-prepared cars after the station was tipped off that the shops may be using deceptive sales practices.

Before sending them to the shops, the cars received new brakes and tune-ups, then they were triple-checked by a diagnostic center, a dealership, and a mechanic/service advisor to make sure no repairs were needed. Reporters then drove the cars to the shops for their advertised $16 oil change and free brake inspection.

According to Channel 2 reporters, many unnecessary repairs were recommended; some of the recommended repairs were done, including brake jobs with new rotors (even though the car's brakes were in perfect condition). One shop said the rotors were too thin and needed to be replaced, so after giving permission to replace them, the reporters took the rotors to another Goodyear store to have them checked. The second store measured them and said they were fine.

One car visited the same store twice, but with different license plates the second time. On the first visit, reporters said store personnel told them that the shocks and struts were OK, but the clutch was bad. On the second visit, reporters were told the clutch was OK, but the car needed new shocks and struts.

Channel 2 reporters said that during another "trip" to one of the stores for the $16 oil and filter special, their car was given a tune-up, even though they hadn't authorized it. When the mechanic noticed that the car already had new spark plugs, and told the manager, reporters said he was told to tune it anyway.

The results of the investigation were aired on TV, using the title, "Taken for a Ride." When they were interviewed, Goodyear company officials said they didn't know those things were going on; they also said they would investigate and take action if they found a problem.

It turned out that the store personnel were on a sales incentive (commission) program, and when company officials were asked if they would discontinue it because of the current problems, they said they didn't know. They also said that [sales commission for mechanics] was the common pay practice for the industry.

As a result of the Channel 2 show, the state Attorney General started its own investigation of Goodyear company stores. Current and former store employees were interviewed regarding company sales practices, and a settlement was reached in December of 1993. Goodyear agreed to discontinue its product-specific and service-specific incentive programs, pay for arbitration in disputes about the sale of unnecessary or unauthorized repairs, establish safeguards, and contribute $40,000 for consumer education.

Undercover Investigation, 1993-94
Goodyear Auto Centers, Illinois

In November 1993, Channel 5 (WMAQ-TV) in Chicago started an undercover investigation similar to the one done in 1992 by Channel 2 (KSTP-TV) in Minnesota. The undercover cars were put in "top-running condition" by a master mechanic, then they were triple-checked by a AAA consultant for the Chicago Motor Club and a diagnostic company. Once again, the targets were Goodyear company-owned stores.

Reporters for Unit 5 took the cars to company-owned Goodyear Auto Centers in Chicago, asking for full inspections at 13 different stores. At 6 of the stores, Unit 5 said mechanics recommended a variety of services, including tune-ups (with new caps and wires), brake jobs (with new rotors), transmission services, shocks, tires, struts, and cooling system flushes. Reporters authorized some of the recommended services and received bills for $485...$297...$652...for repairs on cars already in "top-running condition," cars that even the other 7 Goodyear stores claimed did not need any work.

Four mechanics from one of the offending stores (and one recently-fired mechanic) went on record with their explanations: "Get all the money. They're not worried about the customer." (John)..."I've been told to do service that doesn't need it." (Dave)..."People are getting ripped-off." (Ken)..."Anything that might make them more money...Fair or unfair." (Jeff)

Unit 5 had copies of Goodyear's sales incentive programs, which explained why some mechanics may have been selling unnecessary repairs. Company memos were found with the following headings: "Special Report," War Update," and "Alert, Alert." Stores were grouped together for competition, and prizes were offered for the most sales. Those with the highest sales were called "top guns," followed by "hand grenades." "Squirt guns" came in last.

Company officials said that the auto repair industry is based on commissions and those were no more than routine sales incentives. They also said the company has safeguards to protect the consumer, including a whistle-blower hot-line, training programs, and requiring employees to sign agreements promising not to sell unnecessary repairs. Goodyear said they do not tolerate the sale of unnecessary repairs and promised to investigate the allegations, even though they disputed them.

As a result of the Unit 5 undercover operation, the Cook County State's Attorney and the Illinois Attorney General have started their own investigations. No doubt fearing further erosion in consumer confidence (and company revenue) from the press coverage of the investigations, Goodyear announced the end of its sales commission program for mechanics on June 1, 1994. The company also said its technicians will receive a higher base pay, and it put into place a new safeguard, the "Customer Trust" program. (See Chapter 19 for details.)

The following sections describe parts and services that are commonly sold as additional repairs by tire & alignment shops. Some of the more common dishonest sales tactics are described, and guidelines are given to help determine whether the additional repairs are really needed.

Valve Stems

The valve stems used 15-20 years ago would usually deteriorate severely if they were not replaced every time new tires were installed (the ozone in the air would cause the rubber stems to crack). However, the rubber used in high-quality valve stems today is far more resistant to ozone, so they do last a lot longer than the old ones did.

If you're only getting 20-25,000 miles out of your tires and the valve stems show no signs of deterioration or other damage, it's not normally necessary to replace them every time new tires are installed; the stems should be good for the life of two tires (40-50,000 miles). However, if your tires are lasting 40-50,000 miles, it's probably a good idea to replace the valve stems every time the tires are changed. New valve stems only cost a couple of dollars (each), and since they probably won't last 80-100,000 miles (the life of two tires), it's a good idea to change them when the new tires are installed.

Ball Joints

Ball joints are ball and socket assemblies that connect the

steering knuckle to the control arms, allowing the knuckle to rotate so the vehicle can be steered. Ball joints that are excessively worn will cause the front end to be "loose" or "sloppy," thereby preventing an accurate alignment. Also, excessively worn ball joints that are not replaced for a long time (sometimes months, sometimes years, depending on the vehicle and driving conditions) can separate, causing loss of steering control.

A vehicle shouldn't need two or three ball joint jobs during its lifetime--most vehicles will only need to have the ball joints replaced once, if at all. Unlike shocks and brakes, ball joints don't have to be replaced in pairs. Don't let a dishonest shop sell you unnecessary repairs--if only one ball joint is bad, only one has to be replaced.

Some mechanics use a "hard sell" to convince a customer that his ball joints should be replaced because the rubber boots on the ball joints are torn. They claim that the ball joints will quickly fail because a tear in a boot will cause all of the grease to leak out, allowing contamination to enter the joint.

This claim is basically true, but the urgency is often exaggerated. The grease used to lubricate front suspensions is fairly thick, so it won't just run out of a tear in a boot. Depending on the climate and driving conditions, a ball joint with a torn boot may last anywhere from several months to several years before it becomes so worn that replacement is necessary. (The less severe the driving conditions and the more frequently the ball joint is lubricated, the longer it will last.)

Most tire and alignment shops love to sell ball joint jobs because they are a relatively high-dollar (and high-profit) item. A mechanic who has done a lot of ball joint jobs can usually complete the job in less time than the flat rate books allow, making the shop even more money.

Several dishonest tactics have been used to pressure

reluctant customers into buying this expensive repair. The first tactic is to tell a customer who has just purchased new tires that the tire warranty will be void if the ball joints are not replaced, because they will cause premature tread wear. (This is not necessarily true, as already explained in the beginning of this chapter.)

The second tactic used is "showing" the customer how bad the ball joints really are. The customer is taken into the shop where a mechanic with a long bar is prying on the tire or steering knuckle to show the customer how "loose" the ball joints are. Any movement in the ball joint is exaggerated by the use of a long pry bar--the proper way to check the ball joints for excessive wear is to grab the tire at the top and bottom, and to rock the tire using your hands, not a long pry bar. (The vehicle must first be jacked up to remove coil spring pressure on the ball joint being checked.)

It's not necessarily true that any movement in a ball joint indicates excessive wear. All vehicle manufacturers have their own specifications for allowable movement; a one-sixteenth inch movement might be acceptable on one vehicle but not on another.

If you are being shown how "bad" your ball joints are, insist that they measure all movement with a dial indicator and record the reading on the repair order (this is required by law in California). Ask them what is acceptable according to the factory specification. (If you're still suspicious, ask to see the measurement and the specification for yourself.)

A situation that existed on certain Ford vehicles built in the 1960's and 1970's is a good illustration of how widespread the sale of unnecessary ball joint repairs has been. These vehicles had original-equipment upper ball joints that were spring-loaded and had a normal vertical movement of one-quarter inch. Although they appeared to be "loose," these ball joints did not require replacement if the vertical movement was only one-quarter inch or less.

Since this movement was considerably more than that found on other vehicles, many mechanics sold their customers new ball joints, installing a different brand that was not spring-loaded (and had no vertical movement at all). By showing the customer how "loose" their original ball joints were, and comparing them to ball joints on another vehicle (or to the new ones after they were installed), the customer was convinced that replacement was necessary, even though it wasn't.

This sale of unnecessary front end repairs, especially ball joints, was so common that the California Bureau of Automotive Repair worked with several district attorneys' offices to conduct undercover "sweeps" of suspect shops. These shops were chosen because they had an excessive number of similar consumer complaints.

The investigation revealed that too many unnecessary ball joint repairs were being done, so permanent injunctions were entered against many of the shops requiring them to use a dial indicator to measure the ball joint movement before replacement is recommended. Also, the test results must be recorded on the repair order.

Idler Arms

An idler arm is a rotating bracket that is attached to the frame to support the steering linkage. If the idler arm bushing becomes excessively worn, it will allow the steering linkage to move up and down, causing the alignment to change (it will also make it impossible to align the front end properly).

Since idler arm replacement is easy and profitable, it is the most frequently-sold front end part. Beware of mechanics using a long pry bar on the idler arm to show how "loose" it is--even a new one will move if enough force is applied to it.

The proper way to check an idler arm for wear is to pull or push on the outer end with your hand, applying only moderate pressure. If there is a noticeable movement (one thirty-second of an inch or more, measured at the outer end), it should be compared with the specification in the manual. The idler arm should be replaced if the movement is greater than the specification listed.

A new idler arm will not usually have any movement in the bushing, but one that has been on the vehicle for a long time may have a slight amount of play in it without affecting the front end alignment. However, if it does have a slight amount of play in the bushing, this is usually an indication that the bushing is starting to wear out and will need to be checked or replaced at a later date.

How long an idler arm like this will last before it has to be replaced depends on the vehicle and driving conditions. I've seen idler arms with one thirty-second of an inch movement that took a year to develop any more play in the bushing, but if the vehicle is continuously driven over rough roads, it may only be a month or two before it gets worse.

If your vehicle is in the shop for tires or alignment, and you are told that it needs a new idler arm, ask them to show you the specification and how loose it is. Make sure they are only using their hands to pull or push on the idler arm, not a pry bar. If you can hardly see any movement, it probably doesn't need to be replaced. On some GM models (1974 and later with rear wheel drive, for example), up to one-eighth of an inch movement is normal, so make sure they check the specification in the manual.

Note: If you have a late-model vehicle with rack and pinion steering (most front wheel drives and other small cars), it doesn't have an idler arm, so if someone tries to sell you one, he's either extremely dishonest or extremely incompetent.

Tie Rod Ends

Tie rod ends are part of the steering linkage that connect the rack and pinion (or the center steering link) to the steering knuckles (at the front wheels). Sockets in the tie rod ends allow them to rotate when the wheels are turned. If the sockets become worn, the steering linkage will become sloppy, and it will be impossible to align the front end properly.

If a tire & alignment shop tells you that your tie rod ends need to be replaced, ask them to show you how bad they are. Make sure they are not using a pry bar to show you how "loose" the ends are--that will only exaggerate any movement.

The proper way to check tie rod ends is to pull or push on them with your hands, using moderate force. A lever or pry bar is unnecessary--a bad tie rod end will be noticeably loose when it is checked by hand. Other than side-to-side rotation of the socket (which is normal), it should be fairly tight. On most vehicles, if the tie rod end socket is loose (i.e. it can be pushed in and out by hand), it is probably worn out. Before replacing any ends, check the manufacturer's specifications for allowable movement--some vehicles in the past had spring-loaded tie rod ends that appeared to be loose when they were actually OK.

An automotive instructor (and former mechanic) that I worked with accompanied a friend to a tire center where he was getting new tires and an alignment. The mechanic told his friend that his car needed new tie rod ends and proceeded to demonstrate how "loose" they were by rotating the ends in the sockets.

His friend was lucky to have someone with him who had an automotive background, because he knew nothing at all about cars. Normally, he would have believed the mechanic and had the tie rod ends replaced, but the instructor told him that the ends are supposed to rotate like that; there was nothing wrong with them.

I can't believe that was just an honest mistake--no front end mechanic could be that incompetent! Which just goes to show that there are unscrupulous mechanics out there, and consumers need to be careful to avoid paying for unnecessary repairs.

Some shops really push the sale of new tie rod ends if the rubber boots are torn, claiming that all of the grease will leak out, resulting in premature failure. This is definitely true if the tie rod end is sealed with no grease fitting, but if it has a fitting and is lubricated regularly, it may last months (or years) before it fails. (The less severe the driving conditions and the more frequently the tie rod end is lubricated, the longer it will last.)

Control Arm Bushings

The control arm bushings connect the control arm to the shaft, and are usually made of rubber mounted between two metal sleeves. As the bushings age, the rubber deteriorates. At first, cracks form in the rubber. The bushing will eventually fall apart if it isn't replaced, resulting in metal-to-metal contact between the control arm and the shaft. If the bushings are loose due to shrinkage or deterioration, it will be impossible to properly align the front end.

Small cracks in the outer edges of the bushings are normal--they are not grounds for replacement. After the cracks are first noticed, the bushings should be inspected periodically until the cracks become deep or the bushings become loose. When this happens, the bushings should be replaced. (It usually takes at least a year after the small cracks appear for the bushings to deteriorate enough that replacement becomes necessary.)

Coil Springs

The coil springs support the weight of the vehicle, and are also used to absorb road impact. Almost all vehicles use coil springs on the front, and many also use them on the rear (instead of leaf springs).

Normally, coil springs don't wear out unless the vehicle is very old or has been used to carry heavy loads. Replacement is usually only necessary if the vehicle leans to one side or if one end of the vehicle is significantly higher than the other.

Before new springs are installed to correct the height of a vehicle, the tire pressure should be checked (because a vehicle will lean towards the side with a low tire) and the riding height of the vehicle should be measured. That measurement should be compared with the factory specifications found in suspension manuals. (Any shop that does alignments or suspension work should have these manuals.)

The specifications usually allow for a slight deviation, eliminating guesswork that often results in unnecessary repairs. If no deviation is given, the coil springs shouldn't be replaced unless there is a significant difference (a half-inch or more) between the specification and the actual vehicle measurement. (A deviation of one-quarter inch is only one or two percent of the total riding height measurement on most vehicles.)

Some shops really push the sale of coil springs, especially for the rear of the vehicle. Rear coil springs are usually very easy to replace, allowing the shop to complete a $100-150 job in a matter of minutes. Front springs usually take at least an hour or two to replace, so they are not pushed as much.

Shock Absorbers & (MacPherson) Struts

"Shock absorber" is a slightly misleading name for this part, since the springs actually absorb the initial shock when the vehicle hits a bump. A more accurate name for this part would be "bounce absorber," because the shocks are actually designed to prevent the suspension from continuous bouncing after going over a bump. They also prevent the vehicle from leaning excessively to one side when cornering. MacPherson struts are simply shock absorbers mounted inside the coil spring assemblies.

Occasionally a shock will bind up, preventing the spring from being compressed and absorbing the initial shock, resulting in a very rough ride. However, the most common signs of worn shocks are fluid leaking past the shock seals, excessive bouncing after driving over bumps, and/or excessive leaning when cornering. Also, a loss of steering control may be experienced after driving over a bump.

If your vehicle is in the shop and you are told that it needs new shocks, ask them to tell you (and show you) why your shocks need to be replaced. The following conditions are legitimate grounds for replacement:

1. One of the shocks is binding (it won't compress or extend easily).
2. One of the shocks is leaking, bent, or dented.
3. The tires have a scalloped wear pattern along the outer edges (that is not caused by out-of-balance

wheels).
4. The shocks fail the "bounce test."

The "bounce test" should be used to check for worn shocks that are not leaking or otherwise physically damaged. Park the vehicle on a level, even surface--not over a lift or hoist (because the bottom of the vehicle may hit when it is bounced).

Push down as hard as you can on one corner of the vehicle (or better yet, have the mechanic do this while you watch), then release it and watch how many times the vehicle goes up and down. If necessary, repeat at the other corners. A vehicle with good shocks will go up, then part of the way down, and stop. If it goes up, down, then all the way up again, the shocks are worn out and should be replaced.

MacPherson struts are more difficult to check than normal shocks. Because they are located inside the coil spring assembly, it's not usually possible to inspect them visually. The only way to check them is with a bounce test.

Shocks should always be replaced in pairs (both fronts or both rears at the same time). If all of your shocks have been on the vehicle awhile (at least 50,000 miles) and one of them needs to be replaced, it's probably a good idea to replace all of them at the same time, especially if the old ones have been on there since the vehicle was new.

The reason for this is that most replacement shocks are "heavy duty," which means that they are usually more firm than original-equipment ("OEM") shocks. A vehicle that has two new heavy-duty shocks mixed with two OEM shocks will not handle as well as a vehicle with four that are relatively equal.

Some shops routinely push new "heavy-duty" shocks on all customers that have OEM shocks on their vehicles, in spite of the fact that the "old" shocks pass the visual and bounce tests. They falsely claim or imply that the OEM shocks are sub-standard or weak, and should be replaced with new heavy-duty ones. *Don't fall for this scam!*

I have seen mechanics demonstrate how "bad" a customer's shocks were by taking one of them off the vehicle, then compressing it to show how "tired" and worn out it is. Don't fall for this trick--a shock is supposed to compress easily, but offer a lot more resistance when it is being extended. (If shocks were made to have a lot of resistance when they were being compressed, vehicles would have an extremely rough ride--every bump in the road would be felt inside.) It's also normal for a new shock to have more resistance than one that has been on a vehicle for a while; it doesn't necessarily mean that the used shock is worn out.

Don't let someone sell you new shocks just because your old ones have a lot of miles on them. If there are no visible signs of fluid leaks or damage, and they pass the bounce test, they don't need to be replaced. I have seen shocks with 80-90,000 miles on them that still passed the bounce test, showed no signs of leaking or other damage, and were not causing any unusual tire wear.

Wheel Bearings

Rear wheel drive vehicles have two wheel bearings in each front wheel that are serviceable, and one bearing on each rear axle that is not. Front wheel drive vehicles have two wheel bearings in each rear wheel that are serviceable, and one bearing on each front axle that is usually not serviceable.

Serviceable wheel bearings occasionally need to be inspected, cleaned, and repacked with high-quality grease.

At this time, new grease seals should be installed. Normally, if this is done properly when the brakes are relined, they won't need to be serviced again before the next brake job (usually at least 30-40,000 miles). Some shops recommend wheel bearing services every 10-20,000 miles, which I think is unnecessary.

The bearings (and their corresponding races) should be inspected for pitting, scoring, or discoloration, which are signs of overheating and bearing failure. A bearing or race with any of these signs should be replaced. It's not necessary to replace bearings in pairs or sets, so don't let someone tell you that all of them have to be changed just because one of them is bad.

CHAPTER 4

Tune-up Shops

Note: This chapter applies to shops that advertise "quick" tune-ups for $39-49. Many of these shops also offer other minor services such as smog inspections, lube and oil changes, brake jobs, etc., which is sometimes reflected in their name (for example, "ABC Lube & Tune" or "XYZ Tune & Brake"). Most of the well-known shops are individually-owned franchises which benefit from the parent company's advertising, training, and name-recognition.

Have you ever wondered why tune-ups are advertised for $39-49 at one of the "quick tune" shops, when independent repair shops and car dealer service departments charge $80-120? Most people think the dealerships and independent shops charge more because they are greedy, because they have higher profit margins, or because they have higher overhead than the tune-up shops.

Actually, only the last statement is true, but it is not the only reason for the price difference. The other reason is that less work is done on a low-priced tune-up, which is explained later in this chapter.

What is probably the single biggest reason for tune-up shops having lower overhead is that their mechanics are usually paid considerably less than good tune-up technicians working in independent repair shops or dealership service departments. For example, in the city where I live, skilled tune-up and smog technicians can easily get $15-20 (or more) per hour, but most of the mechanics working in the low-priced tune-up shops are only paid $6-10 per hour.

Why are these tune-up shop mechanics paid so much less than technicians working in other repair shops? My guess is that, based on their skill levels and lack of training, they aren't worth any more than what they are being paid. Most of them are basically "parts-changers," not highly-skilled technicians. (If they were highly-skilled, they would probably be working somewhere else for a lot more money.)

The following story is a good illustration of the caliber of mechanics working at many of the low-priced tune-up shops.

I had stopped by a local tune-up shop that was part of a well-known chain to talk to the owner about training for his mechanics. A lady was waiting for them to finish the tune-up on her truck, but she was becoming very irritated because they weren't done yet. They had been working on her truck for two and a half hours, and it was backfiring and running worse than it did before she brought it in.

When they finally told her that nothing else could be done, the lady's patience ran out. She told the manager, "This is ridiculous--you guys have been working on my truck for over two hours, and it runs worse than it did when I brought it in. I want my money back, and I want you to put my old parts back in, so I can take it somewhere else where they know what they're doing."

I was curious as to what they could do to foul up a simple four-cylinder tune-up, so I took a look at the scope and asked the mechanics what they had tried to make it run better. (All three of the "mechanics" on duty were working on it, trying to figure out why it was running poorly.) They said that the timing was too far off, and they couldn't set it because the distributor wouldn't turn any farther.

All they had to do was shut off the engine, pull the distributor out far enough to turn it one tooth, then put it back in, and they would be able to set the timing properly. After wasting two hours, none of the mechanics had tried to do that.

This was such an elementary problem that any apprentice mechanic with six months of tune-up experience should be able to fix it. However, because of their low prices and low pay scales, it's not unusual to find incompetent mechanics at low-priced tune-up shops. In several of the undercover investigations, including the ones outlined in this chapter, the tune-up shops were also charged with doing repairs in an incompetent manner.

Tune-up shops also charge $40-70 less than the other repair shops because they are doing less work and installing fewer new parts. If the ads for cheap tune-ups are examined closely, it becomes obvious that the only new parts they are installing (for the advertised price) are spark plugs.

For example, an actual ad for a well-known tune-up chain reads, "TUNE-UP SPECIAL, 6 CYL. $39.98, Includes: Complete engine analysis; Check fuel & emission systems; Measure exhaust emissions; Install new spark plugs; Inspect filters, belts & PCV; Check & set timing, carburetor & idle speed; 8,000 mile/8 month guarantee, whichever comes first; Standard ignition & Additional parts extra."

Read the ad carefully and you will see that out of six operations that they supposedly perform, only one involves the installation of new parts (the spark plugs). Most of the "checks" and "inspections" that they claim to be doing are nothing more than a quick visual inspection, if they are done at all.

The ads for many tune-up shops claim that their tune-ups only take 30-45 minutes, which would leave little (or no) time for additional "checks" and "inspections" after replacing the spark plugs and making the necessary adjustments. Also, since they are only getting $39-49 for a tune-up, they need to finish the job as fast as possible if they expect to make any money on it. (Because of this, they are often encouraged to save time by doing a less-than-thorough job.)

Personally, I think the ads used by most tune-up shops are very misleading for two reasons: one, because they lead most people to believe that their vehicle only needs a $39-49 tune-up; and two, because many of the mechanics working in those shops do not have the training, knowledge, or equipment required to properly check the ignition, fuel, or emission systems on most late-model vehicles.

Now compare this $39-49 "tune-up" to an $80-120 tune-up done by a dealership or independent repair shop. Their tune-ups typically include the installation of new spark plugs, fuel filter, PCV valve, and rotor (and sometimes an air filter, too) in addition to all of the "checks and adjustments" mentioned in the above ad. Since they are getting paid more money for the tune-up, they have time to do a more thorough job.

After being accused by other mechanics of only "changing spark plugs," the tune-up shops have attempted to defend themselves by claiming that most vehicles don't need more than spark plugs when they are tuned and labeling other tune-ups as "overpriced." By saying this, they are implying that mechanics who replace the fuel filter, PCV valve, and rotor when they tune a vehicle are charging customers for unnecessary parts.

All well-trained journeyman mechanics that I have worked with (and talked to) believe that a proper tune-up requires more than just spark plugs. (I agree.) Even some mechanics working in tune-up shops have admitted that most vehicles do need more than just plugs. In my opinion, any vehicle that can be "properly tuned" for $39-49 probably doesn't need a tune-up in the first place.

If a vehicle only gets cheap tune-ups all the time, the fuel filter, PCV valve, and rotor will never be replaced. When these parts eventually fail (and they will), the vehicle owner will usually be stuck paying for a tow truck as well as diagnostic and repair time, usually at another shop. By the time the problem is diagnosed and repaired, and the rest of the tune-up is checked to make sure it was done properly, failure to replace a fuel filter or rotor during a tune-up could easily result in a towing and repair bill of at least $60-80.

If the PCV valve is never cleaned or replaced, deposits will build up in the valve, reducing the air flow. This will result in reduced gas mileage due to a "richer" fuel mixture. When the PCV valve becomes restricted or plugged, pressure in the crankcase will increase, often resulting in major oil leaks from the engine. I have seen many oil leaks that were greatly reduced (or even eliminated) just by replacing a PCV valve that should have been cleaned or replaced a long time ago.

If the distributor rotor is never replaced, the vehicle may experience driveability problems or a no-start condition when the rotor becomes worn or shorted out.

Most vehicles will develop driveability problems (or even stop running) if the fuel filter is never replaced, because the flow of gas will be restricted or blocked as impurities plug up the filter. Symptoms may include hesitation, lack of power, surging, and/or stalling. On fuel-injected vehicles, a restricted or plugged fuel filter can cause excessive fuel pressure which will damage the electric fuel pump.

I have had to replace many fuel filters and rotors to cure driveability problems or no-start conditions on vehicles that were tuned by well-known tune-up shops. (These items are virtually never changed during a cheap tune-up.) Some of the vehicles had to be towed to our shop because they wouldn't run.

When the owners of the vehicles called the tune-up shops to ask why those parts weren't replaced when the tune-up was done, the shops said they "weren't responsible because those items are not part of our tune-ups." Since most of those vehicles developed problems within 1-2 months of being tuned, it was obvious that those parts should have been part of the tune-up.

Some tune-up shops now realize that many vehicles need to have more than just the spark plugs changed, so they offer "extended-mileage tune-ups." Instead of their normal $39-49 tune-up with an 8 month/8,000 mile guarantee, one well-known tune-up chain is advertising their "12 Month/12,000 Mile Guarantee Tune-up" for $79-89. Their ad states that they will install new spark plugs, rotor, distributor cap, and breather element; all necessary adjustments are included.

Guess what? That's about the same price charged by independent repair shops and dealership service departments for a complete tune-up, including new spark plugs, rotor, PCV valve, and fuel filter. Unfortunately, the "extended mileage tune-ups" at the tune-up shops don't include a new fuel filter or PCV valve, so they're still not what I would consider complete tune-ups.

Here's where I think the tune-up shops are misleading the public. First they advertise what they call "tune-ups" for $39-49, accusing other shops of being "high-priced" for charging more. I think this practice is deceptive, because they fail to tell consumers that their tune-ups are cheaper because they are doing less work and installing fewer new parts. Then they have the nerve to offer an "extended mileage tune-up" for $79-89 (or more), the same level they had previously labeled as "high-priced" when it applied to their competitors.

Their ads also claim that their tune-ups are done by "highly-trained technicians," a statement that could only be true if they are allowed to make up their own definition. If their mechanics really are "highly-trained technicians," why are most of them paid so much less than highly-trained technicians working in independent repair shops and dealership service departments?

Although tune-up shops advertise their low prices, often comparing them to other shops, the low-price policy does not usually apply to additional parts and services that are not included in their basic tune-ups. For example, some of the local tune-up shops have a 70% mark-up on parts (instead of the customary 30-40%) and charge $79.95 for a fuel injection service that is done by many other shops in the area for $50-60.

Abuses have occurred at many tune-up shops in the past. When cheap tune-ups first became popular, almost all of the well-known tune-up chains were claiming that they would "replace the condenser, rotor, cap, fuel filter, and spark plug wires, if necessary" as part of their tune-up (for $50 or less).

Although the tune-up shops would occasionally repair or replace a bad spark plug wire, they practically never replaced any of the other items as part of a tune-up. As a mechanic, I have seen many condensers, rotors, and fuel filters that they should have replaced and didn't. This practice has been discontinued, probably as a result of "truth in advertising" laws.

The pay structure for mechanics used by some of the well-known tune-up chains often encourages the sale of unnecessary parts and services. Mechanics are often paid a low salary (for example, $1,000-1,200 per month) plus commission based on sales of (usually high-priced) additional parts and services. Obviously, the only way their mechanics could make enough to live on would be to sell a lot of additional work.

The following stories illustrate the potential danger concerning low-priced shops that pay their mechanics a low salary plus a sales commission.

Undercover Investigation, 1989-90
Econo Lube N' Tune, California

Five Econo Lube N' Tune shops in Sacramento were charged with performing repairs that were not needed and charging for repairs that were not done. All five shops in the Sacramento area that were charged were franchises owned by the same person.

The state attorney general represented the BAR in an administrative action to suspend or revoke the repair licenses of the franchises. The Bureau had received dozens of complaints against the five shops, and an undercover investigation of them had previously been done.

According to Deputy Attorney General Roy Liebman, undercover vehicles in perfect working order were taken to the shops by BAR agents, who were charged $200 to $300 for repairs in spite of the vehicles' condition. Liebman said the agents requested the $18 oil changes and $39 tune-ups that were advertised, and they were sold various kits, filters, and other parts, none of which was necessary--the shops replaced gas filters that had only been in the car for seven miles, and performed transmission work when overhauls had recently been done.

Liebman also claimed that BAR agents were charged for repairs that were not done. He said the Bureau had put a covert seal on the differential which was still intact after the shop charged the agent for servicing it.

The owner of the franchises was presented with the evidence and entered into negotiations to settle the charges. According to a deputy district attorney working on the case, the Bureau discovered that the shops were still selling unnecessary repairs (even though the owner was negotiating a settlement), so the Bureau filed an action to suspend or revoke the shops' repair licenses.

Shortly after the investigation was publicized, the parent company terminated the franchise agreements for the five shops.

The shops are still in business, but they are now under new ownership. Legal action was still pending against the previous owner, who left the state and was later found working in another chain of "fast-and-cheap" lube, tune, and brake shops in Las Vegas, Nevada.

Undercover Investigation, 1982-84
Quality Tune-Up Shops, California

Note: This undercover bust is fairly old, but it was included anyway for two reasons; one, because some of these tactics are still going on at other low-priced tune-up shops across the country, and two, it's a good illustration of how few consumers realize they were sold unnecessary repairs. Out of the 70,000 people eligible for restitution, only about 125 filed complaints.

The California Bureau of Automotive Repair had received numerous consumer complaints regarding questionable business practices at Quality Tune-Up shops, so an undercover investigation was conducted. When the investigation was completed, a consumer protection lawsuit was filed by the state based on over 100 complaints, 14 undercover operations, and information from 8 ex-employees of the tune-up chain. Out of 40 shops belonging to the chain, 28 were named as defendants.

In the lawsuit, the tune-up shops were charged with selling unneeded spark plug wire sets and electronic ignition sets, using scare tactics to sell unneeded parts, failing to perform repairs in a competent manner, and operating bait and switch schemes.

Quality Tune-Up had been advertising tune-ups for $39.95 to $49.95. According to the deputy attorney general, there was a consistent pattern of customers being told that the tune-up could not be done because the vehicle had faulty ignition (spark plug) wires. He said these customers were then sold electronic ignition sets and wires that added $25-100 to the basic tune-up price.

One of the deputy district attorneys working on the case said that undercover investigators installed new ignition wires (that were treated to look old) on vehicles which were then taken to the shops for tune-ups. He said the investigators were told that their vehicles needed new wires, when the wires actually only had about six miles on them.

He also claimed that the shops used deceptive tests to induce customers to purchase ignition wire sets that were not needed. Customers were allegedly shown the resistance readings of their own wires, then the readings of other new wires that were shorter and made of a different material that had less resistance.

To settle the charges out of court, the Quality Tune-Up shops agreed to pay $430,000 in civil penalties, attorney's fees, and investigative costs. The shops also agreed to make restitution to affected customers in the form of free smog inspections and up to $50 in related repairs.

Up to 70,000 customers were eligible for the free repairs, which would result in total restitution of at least $1.5 million. According to the deputy attorney general, this was the largest automotive repair settlement in the state (at that time) and probably in the country.

The Quality Tune-Up shops were enjoined from the following practices: misrepresenting the results of any test performed on consumer vehicles, offering sales quotas for employees or financially rewarding employees on the basis of sales of electronic ignition wires and sets, selling unneeded spark plug wire sets and electronic ignition sets, using scare tactics to sell unneeded parts, failing to perform repairs in a competent manner, and operating bait and switch schemes.

TUNE-UP GUIDELINES

Older vehicles with ignition points (typically 1974 or earlier) usually need a tune-up every 10-15,000 miles. On these models, the points, condenser, and plugs should be replaced during every tune-up, with the fuel filter, PCV valve*, and rotor being replaced every other time (unless vehicle or driving conditions require more frequent replacement). Many vehicles will need a new air filter and breather element at this time. The distributor cap should be checked at every tune-up and replaced if necessary.

Vehicles with electronic ignition, but without computer controls (typically 1975-79 on GM models, 1975-83 on others) usually need a tune-up every 17-22,000 miles. This should include replacement of the spark plugs, fuel filter, rotor, and PCV valve*. Check the air filter and breather element between tune-ups and replace if necessary. The distributor cap should be checked at every tune-up and replaced if necessary.

Late-model vehicles with computer controls (typically 1980 or later on GM models, 1983 or later on others) usually need a tune-up every 25-30,000 miles. This should include replacement of the spark plugs, fuel filter, rotor, and PCV valve*. The distributor cap should be checked at every tune-up and replaced if necessary. Check the air filter and breather element between tune-ups and replace if necessary.

*On most vehicles, if the PCV valve is cleaned every time the engine is tuned, replacement is not usually necessary.

Insist on the use of high-quality, name-brand parts. After all necessary parts have been replaced, the engine should be tested on an analyzer to make sure no other problems exist and to adjust the timing, idle speed, and air/fuel ratio, if necessary. Expect to pay at least $80-90 for this service, and beware of "cheap tune-up shops" offering to do the job for $39-49.

Vehicles with fuel injection may need to have the injectors professionally cleaned every 30-50,000 miles (at a cost of $50-70). In spite of what the commercials say, using a particular brand of gasoline may not keep all fuel injectors perfectly clean. If your fuel-injected vehicle has quite a few miles on it, and it isn't starting or running as well as it did before, it may need to have the injectors cleaned to restore performance. Ask your technician if he thinks your vehicle would benefit from this service.

One last tip: If your engine is running rough, don't tell the repair shop that it needs a tune-up. Instead, tell them it's running rough and you want them to check it out. It may only need a spark plug wire that costs about $7, or it may need major engine work that a tune-up won't fix. In either case, tuning the engine would be a waste of money.

CHAPTER 5

Transmission Shops

The typical vehicle owner doesn't think about his transmission until he notices that it's no longer working properly. Then, filled with fear that repairs are going to cost hundreds of dollars, he does what he has been conditioned to do (by advertising)--he takes his vehicle to a well-known transmission shop.

Expecting the worst, he is not disappointed. However, instead of the $300-500 estimate he had feared, he is shocked to receive one for $800-900 (or more). Although his vehicle was driveable when he brought it to the shop to find out why it wasn't shifting properly, he is told that the transmission needs a complete overhaul.

Does his transmission really need a complete overhaul, or could it be repaired in the vehicle for considerably less money? Is he being ripped off? Possibly. Not all transmission problems require an overhaul.

How can consumers be sure they're not being sold unnecessary repairs? There is no foolproof way, but the safest method is to choose a reputable, highly-skilled mechanic (or repair shop) using the guidelines in this book instead of choosing a shop because of its advertising or low prices. (For more details, see the chapter titled, "Finding Mechanics You Can Trust.")

This chapter is divided into two parts, manual transmissions and automatic transmissions, because they require different types of maintenance and repairs. Also, more unnecessary repairs have been done on automatic transmissions, so more caution is required when service or repairs are needed.

MANUAL TRANSMISSIONS

Your transmission suddenly becomes hard to shift, so you take it to a well-known transmission shop. After all, you've seen their ads everywhere, and they are transmission specialists, right? You figure all it needs is a minor adjustment or repair, and it will be as good as new, so you leave your vehicle at the shop for an estimate.

When the shop finally calls, they tell you that your vehicle needs a transmission overhaul and a new clutch. It's going to cost $900. After the initial shock wears off, you wonder--are you being ripped off?

The answer depends on whether their diagnosis was correct in the first place and what type of transmission it is. It's not always necessary to rebuild a transmission to cure shifting problems--the solution could be as simple as a loose shifter bolt.

If the transmission will only go into gear when the engine isn't running, it may only need a new clutch master or slave cylinder, or it may need a new clutch. A bad clutch (that isn't releasing completely) can also cause hard shifting or grinding when changing gears.

Hard shifting or lock-up in gear can be caused by a loose or missing shifter bolt, improper shift linkage adjustment, bent shift rod levers, or shift rod lock pins that were incorrectly installed or have fallen out. On many vehicles, these problems can be repaired without removing or rebuilding the transmission.

Some models have a removable shift cover, making it possible to inspect the inside of the transmission and repair the shift mechanism without removing it from the vehicle. On models that don't have this feature, it may be necessary to remove and disassemble the transmission to correct any internal problems.

Beware of shops that say a transmission needs to be rebuilt before they've done an inspection. If internal repairs (or overhaul) are necessary, the transmission must be disassembled before an accurate, final estimate can be given.

If your transmission needs to be rebuilt, and several expensive "hard parts" are needed (for example, gears or shafts that cost over $100 each), it may be a lot cheaper to install an exchange transmission than to repair the one that was in your vehicle. Be sure to ask if this option is available before bringing your vehicle in for major repairs.

When your transmission acts up, don't take it to a transmission shop just because they do a lot of advertising--take the time to locate a reputable, highly-skilled transmission mechanic. If you don't, you may end up paying $800-900 for a transmission overhaul and a new clutch when all it really needed was a new bolt in the shifter.

If you have found a reputable repair shop with well-trained mechanics, but they don't do transmission work, ask them to recommend a good transmission shop. Most mechanics know which shops in their area can be trusted to do an honest, high-quality job.

AUTOMATIC TRANSMISSIONS

Whether your vehicle only needs routine service or major repairs, don't choose a particular transmission shop just because you've seen or heard their advertisements. The large chains of transmission shops advertise heavily to convince people that their shops will do the best job. They also lead people to believe that they will receive the same treatment at all of their shops, but practically all of them are individually-owned franchises, so that's not necessarily true.

Most shops are basically honest, but that still leaves quite a few shops out there that routinely sell unnecessary repairs. Some of these are individually-owned franchises that are part of well-known chains, so name-recognition is no guarantee that you'll get an honest deal at all of their shops.

Beware of shops offering to do transmission services for an unusually-low price (for example, $15-25 instead of the normal $40-60), or free inspections. These tactics are often used by shops guilty of illegal "bait and switch" practices--as soon as they get a vehicle in for an advertised special, they tell the owner that the service can't be done (or that it would be a waste of time and money) because the transmission needs major repairs or an overhaul.

A shop can't make any money on a $15-25 transmission service, so why would they offer to do them at that price? Because they hope to sell a lot of (usually high-priced) repair work to the people who come in for the advertised special. This is often a "come-on" used to sell unnecessary transmission overhauls.

Some shops also sell unnecessary overhauls to cure problems that only require minor repairs. John, a friend of mine who has done transmission work for ten years, told me the following story that is a good example of this. (Compare this story with those in the undercover investigation section.)

An elderly lady left her car at a shop to have the transmission checked because it would not shift out of first gear. They told her that her transmission needed a complete overhaul, which would cost $780. To her credit, she told them not to do any repairs, then she took it to a different shop (where John was working) for another estimate.

When John started her car, he could hear a "hissing" sound coming from the transmission area, so he raised her car on a hoist for a visual inspection. What he found was the cause of the "hissing" sound and the no-shift condition--a disconnected vacuum hose at the transmission modulator.

Since the old hose was not in very good condition (that's why it came off), John installed a new one. After that, he road-tested the car and the transmission worked perfectly. He didn't even charge her for fixing her car (it only took about ten minutes, plus he wanted to show her that there are honest mechanics). She was thrilled!

Was the first shop trying to sell her unnecessary repairs, or was it just an honest mistake? I doubt if it was a mistake. That particular problem is so common, and so easy to check, that any mediocre mechanic should have found it quickly (that's why some investigators use that particular problem in undercover investigations). If it was a mistake, then that mechanic is so incompetent that he should not be allowed to work on cars.

Beware of shops that advertise transmission overhauls at unusually-low prices. The following story illustrates the dangers of going to the shop with the lowest prices in town.

A few years ago, when I was working in an independent repair shop, there was a local transmission shop that advertised overhauls for $249 (complete--parts and labor). I assumed they were actually doing an overhaul and wondered how they could do it for one-half the price charged by other shops. Then one day I discovered their secret.

One of their overhaul customers (or more accurately, "victims") brought her car to our shop to repair a transmission leak. When we asked why she didn't take her car back to have them fix it for free, she said they had already worked on it several times and refused to do any more work without charging her for it.

With her car up on a hoist, we did a quick visual inspection. The transmission looked like it had been rebuilt--the outside had been thoroughly cleaned and painted. However, when we removed the pan to repair the leak, we discovered the secret of their incredibly low prices--they had not overhauled the transmission.

Instead of overhauling a transmission, they would only repair the one part that had failed. Then they would clean and paint the outside of the transmission to make it look like it had been overhauled, and charge the customer for an overhaul that was never done. That lady's transmission kept leaking because that shop had not replaced all of the seals.

It wouldn't be fair to suggest that all shops offering to do low-priced services intend to sell unnecessary repairs, but since that tactic is so commonly used by dishonest "bait and switch" repair shops, it's safer to avoid those specials completely rather than running the risk of becoming a victim.

Sometimes an overhaul is necessary to cure what seems like a minor problem, especially if the transmission was low on fluid or slipping for a while before it was brought in for repairs. When the fluid level is too low or slipping occurs, excessive friction and heat are created which can quickly destroy the transmission. Fluid that is discolored or smells burnt indicates that the transmission was overheated and seriously damaged.

If a vehicle is brought in for repair immediately after a problem develops, it's often possible to repair the transmission without an overhaul. This is especially true if it had been properly maintained (i.e., the fluid was changed regularly and never got burnt).

Most fluid leaks can be fixed without removing the transmission from the vehicle. However, it is necessary to remove the transmission to replace the front seal. As long as the transmission was properly maintained and no slippage occurred, it is not usually necessary to overhaul it to repair leaks.

Other common problems that can sometimes be repaired without an overhaul include: failure to shift to a higher or lower gear, slipping when shifting to a higher gear, and starting out in second gear when the shifter is in "Drive."

Regular maintenance of an automatic transmission will greatly reduce the likelihood of expensive repairs being needed before the vehicle has at least 100,000 miles on it. Most transmission specialists recommend servicing every 15-30,000 miles, depending on driving conditions. Servicing should include fluid and filter change, band adjustment, and inspection.

If your vehicle needs a transmission service, take it to a transmission shop or a regular repair shop. *Don't take it to one of the "fast and cheap" lube and oil shops.* The workers in lube and oil shops generally have no experience or knowledge of automatic transmissions, so they wouldn't be able to perform any of the inspections or adjustments that should be done when a transmission is serviced.

During a one-year period, a transmission mechanic that I know had to repair several automatic transmissions that had been serviced by a local lube and oil shop. They failed to tighten all of the filter screws inside the transmission and some of the screws fell out. Those loose screws caused the gears to jam, resulting in cracked transmission cases. In order to repair those transmissions, they had to be rebuilt with new cases at a cost of $700-$1,000.

It may be too late to start servicing a transmission if it hasn't been done for at least 50-60,000 miles. Servicing it at this point could cause leaks to develop, or even complete transmission failure, if the accumulated varnish that is preventing seals from leaking is cleaned out. It may be safer not to service it, and to just drive it until the transmission needs an overhaul.

If you take your vehicle to a transmission shop for routine service or major repairs, and you're not sure that they are completely honest, be sure to wait at the shop while they remove the transmission pan.

The pan must be removed to make an inspection and give an estimate for repairs. Even if you had no problems with the transmission and only brought it in for a routine service, they could find an excessive amount of metal or clutch material in the pan, indicating the need for major repairs. Beware of shops that give repair estimates without removing the pan for inspection, especially if they say your transmission needs to be rebuilt.

There are two important reasons for you to watch while they remove the pan: one, so you can see for yourself if there really is excessive metal or clutch material in the pan; and two, to make sure the pan they are showing you came from your vehicle (and not from someone else's that was a lot worse than yours). If you weren't watching, an unscrupulous mechanic could put metal in your pan or show you the metal in someone else's pan, and you wouldn't even know it.

A thin film of gray material in the pan is normal.

Large (i.e. easily noticeable) metal particles or piles of clutch material usually indicate major problems, even though the transmission may have worked fine before it was brought in. On some Chrysler Torqueflite transmissions, however, heavy deposits in the pan may be normal if the vehicle has quite a few miles on it.

An honest transmission shop won't object to a customer waiting at the shop and watching while the pan is removed for inspection. (Due to insurance regulations, they probably won't allow you to stay inside the shop, but you can usually watch them remove the pan from outside.)

Beware of shops that object to your waiting and watching while they remove the pan. If they start making excuses about why you shouldn't (or can't) wait and watch, you should take your vehicle somewhere else for inspection and repairs.

It's not always possible to give an accurate, final estimate for a transmission overhaul before it is completely disassembled. Most estimates given before disassembly include labor and "soft parts" (gaskets, seals, clutches) only.

When the transmission is disassembled, they may discover that some "hard parts" (gears, drums, converter, etc.) are worn and need to be replaced. One new hard part (for example, a gear) can cost over $100, so a revised estimate can be considerably higher than the original one.

Don't automatically assume that you are being ripped off because they call after taking your transmission apart to tell you that it's going to cost more than they originally thought. An honest, professional shop will always warn customers of this possibility before any work is done, so beware of shops that fail to tell you this up front.

If your transmission is in really bad shape (i.e., it was slipping for a long time, or the fluid is badly burnt), it may be a lot cheaper to install an exchange transmission than to repair the one in your vehicle. Be sure to ask if this option is available before bringing your vehicle in for major repairs.

UNDERCOVER INVESTIGATIONS

AAMCO TRANSMISSIONS--
California, Iowa, Louisiana, Massachusetts, Michigan, Missouri, New Jersey, New York, North Carolina, Ohio, Pennsylvania, Tennessee, Texas, Utah, Washington, West Virginia, Wisconsin

BACKGROUND--
On December 17, 1970, the Federal Trade Commission obtained a consent order barring Aamco Transmissions, Inc. from using deceptive practices in the repair and rebuilding of automotive transmissions. In the order, Aamco was prohibited from the following:

Misrepresenting products or services to obtain leads for major transmission repairs.

Furnishing others [franchisees] with deceptive advertising material.

Promising "one day service" when it is not available. In December 1981, a civil suit filed by the State of California against Aamco and eighteen of its franchisees was settled. The suit was a result of a three-year investigation of Aamco's California franchisees by the Bureau of Automotive Repair. The settlement included payment of $100,000 in civil penalties and investigation costs by nine of the franchisees, in addition to court orders prohibiting Aamco and the franchisees from the unfair practices listed below. (Nine other Aamco franchisees named in the original suit had gone out of business during the settlement negotiations.)

In the suit, Aamco was charged with deceptive advertising because its ads for "free multi-check" and "free road test" did not disclose that a teardown inspection (for which there would be a substantial charge) was necessary to diagnose internal transmission problems. The individual shops were charged with the following:

Recommending or selling unnecessary repairs.

Misrepresenting the condition of customers' transmissions.

Representing or implying that parts or services have been provided when they have not.

Representing or implying that metal particles in a transmission pan indicate a major transmission problem when it is not true and without telling customers that metal particles appear in every transmission pan, even on new vehicles.

In February 1987, a settlement was reached which ended a two-year investigation of Aamco Transmission Centers by the attorneys-general of 14 states. (California, New Jersey, and Utah were not part of this group.) As part of the settlement, Aamco agreed to pay $500,000 to the states for investigation costs. It also agreed to consent orders which prohibit the company and its franchisees from the following:

Using bait-and-switch tactics or other deceptive sales practices.

Misrepresenting that a teardown inspection or other major repairs are required.

Misrepresenting that repairs have been made.

Collecting for repairs that have not been made.

Collecting for repairs which said defendants know or reasonably ought to know are unnecessary.

Refusing to provide estimates before transmissions are disassembled.

Altering parts of customers' motor vehicles with the

intent to create a condition requiring repairs.

The consent decree also ordered the parent company to set up a program to monitor customer complaints, and to take specific action against franchises that receive too many complaints during a six month period. Aamco investigators were to conduct undercover "shopping" runs at franchises receiving three or more complaints in one category. Franchises that failed a "full scale shopping" by recommending and providing unnecessary major internal repairs were to be sold or terminated.

Before the consent decree, Aamco shops would not give estimates to customers until after their transmissions were disassembled, a practice that is now prohibited. Because of this, and the publicity surrounding the investigation and settlement, many Aamco franchisees have reportedly suffered substantial drops in revenue, some as much as 50%.

It appears that the investigation has also caused a significant drop in the number of Aamco shops in the country. Some of the states involved in the investigation claimed that many (or most) of the Aamco shops in their state went out of business shortly after the settlement was publicized. In February 1987, a company spokeswoman stated that the company had 900 locations. In November 1990, the number given by a spokeswoman was "about 700."

What started this multi-state effort that resulted in such drastic changes? Numerous complaints were filed against Aamco with the consumer protection agencies in the 14 states. According to one of the attorneys general who worked on the case, investigators found 2500 instances of customer complaints that they were charged for repairs that weren't requested, weren't needed, or weren't even done. Investigators claimed that many of the complaints concerned Aamco's refusal to honor warranties and repair charges that they called "unconscionable." (Some people were charged as much as $2300 for a transmission overhaul on a GM vehicle that only would have cost $700-800 at most other shops.)

Almost all of the states involved used undercover investigations to build their cases. Agents were fitted with hidden microphones to record statements made by the shops to sell repairs. The cars that were used either had completely rebuilt transmissions or ones that were in perfect working order, except for minor external problems that were created immediately before the car was taken to a suspect shop.

The problems that were created were usually a disconnected vacuum hose at the modulator or misadjusted linkage, both of which would cause shifting problems. Shop manuals and accepted trade practices dictate that those items be checked before any internal repairs are attempted. (Only the most inexperienced or incompetent transmission mechanic would not know this.)

In Missouri, undercover agents shopped five St. Louis Aamco stores a total of fifteen times, using three different cars with completely rebuilt transmissions. Sometimes the modulator hose was disconnected before they went to the stores, but other times the transmission was in perfect working order with no symptoms. The agents claimed that complete overhauls were recommended and sold thirteen times out of the fifteen visits. According to the attorney general's office, there were twenty-one Aamco stores in the state before the investigation was publicized; five of them were closed or sold shortly afterwards.

In Michigan, the Bureau of Auto Regulation conducted the undercover investigation. According to the Bureau, undercover cars with rebuilt transmissions and no problems were sent to shops for routine service (fluid change, etc.), where agents were sold overhauls for $400-

900. Two Aamco stores charged with selling unnecessary repairs were on probation as a result of an earlier investigation; those stores were closed down. There were over twenty Aamco stores in the state before the investigations; now there are only three.

The Michigan Bureau claimed that one of the Aamco stores sabotaged the transmission on an undercover car so it would fail. The agent (who was wearing a wire arranged by the attorney general's office) brought in a car that had a rebuilt transmission and no problems. After the shop serviced the transmission, he was allegedly told that it might start slipping, and that if it did, it would need major repairs. The Bureau said the transmission did start slipping within minutes, because the shop had loosened the band adjustment to make it slip. The shop was charged with sabotage.

In Wisconsin, the investigation started after an Aamco shop manager walked into the office of a Department of Justice investigator to confess. He said his conscience had been bothering him, and he had to tell someone what had been going on at the shop. The shocking story that he revealed was backed up by an ex-mechanic from the shop who testified for the state.

According to the investigator, the Aamco manager documented 95 cases (from the two shops he managed) of customers that were charged for repairs that were unnecessary, or were not even done. The manager said that the shop routinely charged customers for rebuilt torque converters, when the old ones were just cleaned and repainted. (The Justice Department later found four state fleet vehicles that the Aamco shop had supposedly put rebuilt converters in, but had actually just repainted them.)

The Aamco manager told of one instance involving a manual transmission that had been disassembled for an inspection, but had nothing wrong with it. However, the shop owner told the customer that the bearings were bad, and when the customer told him to save the old bearings, the shop owner instructed the mechanic to ruin the bearings with a torch. The customer was then told that the bearings were so bad that they had to be cut out with a torch. (The shop foreman also testified that this story was true.)

According to the investigator, there were ten Aamco shops in Wisconsin before the investigation and consent decree were publicized; now there is only one.

Did the 1987 investigation and consent order put an end to allegations of unlawful and fraudulent business practices at Aamco shops? While investigators admit that the number of complaints has dropped dramatically, they have not dried up completely. (With 200 fewer Aamco stores now than there were in 1987, and the new requirement to give written estimates before doing a teardown inspection, the number of complaints should have dropped.)

SINCE 1987--
In California, several Aamco franchises have been investigated by the Bureau of Automotive Repair and charged with unlawful and/or fraudulent business practices.

The New Jersey Attorney General's office started an undercover investigation of several Aamco shops in August 1989. A civil suit was then filed charging them with selling unnecessary repairs. To settle the charges, the shops paid civil fines and agreed to consent decrees prohibiting them from using unlawful business practices.

In March 1990, five Aamco franchise owners filed suit in federal court against Aamco Transmissions, Inc., claiming that senior Aamco officers have threatened and harassed shop owners to prevent them from exposing a company scheme to defraud customers.

Aamco claimed that the five were trying to ruin the company's reputation and encourage other shop owners to renege on their franchise agreements. Some franchisees had taken sides with the five who filed the lawsuit, while others had sided with the parent company.

The five Connecticut shop owners accused Aamco of encouraging some franchisees to perform unnecessary repairs to increase revenues. In the lawsuit, they made the following accusations:

> "The basic and constant scheme is to lure customers into Aamco franchises...cause them to believe they have a major internal transmission problem, then get them to authorize removal and disassembly of the transmission." "Finally, when the transmission is disassembled and [customers] are at a bargaining disadvantage, [the Aamco representative offers] them only the choice of either a fully rebuilt transmission at prices significantly above the competitive market price, or having no work done and having the transmission reassembled for a substantial price."

In the lawsuit, they accused Aamco of allowing some franchise owners to stay in business despite a history of fraud. (If this is true, it would be a violation of the consent orders that Aamco signed in 1987.) The documents identified 58 franchisees who allegedly used unlawful and/or fraudulent business practices.

Despite investigations by state and federal authorities, the five claimed in the lawsuit that the alleged scheme to defraud consumers has continued.

The franchisees later dropped their lawsuit against the parent company. When asked about the claims made by his clients in the suit, their attorney said, "The parties have amicably resolved their differences and don't believe any purpose would be served by any further comment."

Undercover Investigation, 1987
Lee Myles Transmissions, Arizona

Three independently-owned Lee Myles Transmission shops were the subjects of an undercover investigation by the Arizona Attorney General's office. The investigation was done in response to numerous consumer complaints that had been filed against the three shops.

The attorney general's office claimed that the shops had run continuous ads for low-priced transmission services (from $4.95 to $9.95) to attract customers, then when the services were being done, they would show the customers the metal particles in the pan (which were normal), tell the customers the fluid was burnt, and get them to initial the form giving permission to do a teardown inspection.

Investigators said that customers were not given estimates before their transmissions were disassembled. The shops allegedly told people that they didn't have any idea how much repairs would cost without disassembling the transmission. Investigators claimed that after a transmission was taken apart, in almost all cases the shops told customers that major repairs were needed.

Undercover cars with completely rebuilt transmissions were sent to the shops; the agents were wired to record what was said. To create a problem requiring repairs, a hole was punched in the rear seal, causing it to leak. (Since the transmissions were already thoroughly rebuilt, the only repair that was needed was a new rear seal. Including parts and labor, this would normally cost about $50.)

The following story of what allegedly happened at one

of the shops was taken from the investigator's notes and the recording that was made from the undercover wire.

> Warren Poole [the undercover agent] took the car to the Indian School Road shop on June 29, 1987, and told "Chip" [a shop employee] that the transmission was leaking. After an external examination was performed, "Chip" told Poole that various parts of the transmission were leaking (in addition to the rear seal) and that there was metal in the transmission pan which meant that something was breaking up inside. "Chip" told Warren the transmission had a "problem," and that it needed to be taken apart and inspected (for a charge of $150, which would be credited toward the repair cost if the repairs were done at that shop). Poole asked how much the repairs would cost and "Chip" assured Poole that "It's not gonna be that costly."
>
> After the transmission was taken apart, "Chip" told Poole that a number of parts were damaged and that the total cost of repairs needed was $791.33. The work was done and Poole did in fact pay $791.33 for it. The tape of this undercover is especially interesting, because "Chip" assured Poole at least twice that "We're here to help you, not to rip you off." "Chip" also disparaged other transmission repair shops, saying that "We're not like some transmission places that are out to rip you off" and that "AAMCO stands for 'All Automatics [transmissions] Must Come Out.'"

The attorney general's office filed a civil suit against the three Lee Myles shops (which were all owned by one person), accusing the shops of the following:

Deceptive and fraudulent business practices.

"Bait and switch" practices.

Making promises of free inspections or diagnoses to lure customers to their shops, then refusing to diagnose problems until customers obligated themselves to pay internal inspection fees.

Falsely representing that repairs were necessary.

Falsely representing that parts were installed, and charging for those parts, when they were not installed.

Falsely representing that repairs were performed, and charging for those repairs, when they were not performed.

Representing themselves as "transmission specialists" and "experts," and that they would perform high-quality workmanship, when in fact repair work sold by them was frequently of poor quality.

The parent company (Lee Myles Corp.) was aware of the problems with the owner of the three shops and had been trying to resolve them. When the lawsuit was filed against the franchise owner, the company terminated his franchise agreement. Press releases were issued and ads were placed to inform the public that the company did not approve of the conduct of that franchisee, and that they had terminated his right to do business under the Lee Myles name. One of the company's ads said, "We found something wrong under our hood. So we fixed it...No shortcuts...If it's broken we'll fix it. If it's not, we'll leave it alone. That's a promise."

On December 8, 1988, a superior court judge found the accusations to be true, and ordered the defendants to pay $50,000 for restitution, and $2,500 for civil penalties. (By this time, the defendants had ceased operation of the shops.) All owners, officers, and employees were prohibited from any ownership or employment connected with repairing or servicing motor vehicles for a period of ten years.

Other Undercover Investigations

Independently-owned shops from the following chains have also been charged with unlawful and/or fraudulent business practices in the service and repair of transmissions:

California — Gibraltar Transmissions, Interstate Transmission, Mr. Transmission
Florida -- Aaction Transmissions, Transmission Express, Transmission World, Speedy Transmissions
Michigan -- A-1 Transmissions, American Transmission, Interstate Transmission, Royal Transmission
Missouri -- Cottman Transmissions
New Jersey -- Cottman Transmissions, Lee Myles Transmissions
Tennessee -- Mr. Transmission*
Utah -- Mr. Transmission

*Civil suit filed by attorney general based on numerous complaints against 29 shops; no undercover work done. Case settled--consent order issued.

SUMMARY

It should be obvious after reading this chapter that the area of transmission repairs has more abuses than any other. The alleged acts described in the undercover stories (especially the "confessions" of the Aamco manager, and the Lee Myles case) were outrageous, to say the least, but they were by no means unique. Investigators all across the country have hundreds of similar stories that are documented by undercover tapes and testimonies by former shop employees. Some shop owners and mechanics have even been convicted of criminal fraud and theft as a result of undercover investigations.

Most of the shops were accused of selling rebuilt transmissions to customers who had just come in for a routine service. The shops had been advertising a low-priced transmission service, so many vehicles were brought in that had no problems at all--the people just wanted the fluid changed.

How were these shops able to sell expensive overhauls to people who were not having any problems with their transmissions? Besides making alleged misrepresentations, this was usually done by claiming that they couldn't give estimates until the transmissions were taken out of the vehicles and disassembled. This puts the customer at a serious bargaining disadvantage, which explains why some people paid as much as $2300 for repairs that would have cost $700-800 at most other shops.

Don't fall for this trick! Without disassembling a transmission, any honest transmission shop can give an exact price for a "soft-parts overhaul," which includes all labor to remove, rebuild, and replace the transmission, along with internal clutches, bands, gaskets, seals, and fluid. The only parts that would be additional are "hard parts," which include gears, shafts, drums, etc., that don't normally wear out.

It is necessary to disassemble a transmission to inspect the hard parts, so an estimate for a soft-parts overhaul may be revised upward after disassembly. However, at least you'll know the minimum amount that repairs will cost before your vehicle is taken apart and disabled.

Make sure you get a detailed, written estimate before they touch your vehicle. (When you find out how much it's going to cost, you may tell them to forget it, especially if your transmission worked fine before you brought it in. This will also give you a chance to get a second opinion before any repairs are made, which might save you from being ripped-off.)

If reading this chapter has made you paranoid about taking your car to a shop that does a lot of advertising for low-priced services or free inspections, it should. Now you'll choose a shop the intelligent way--by asking for references from your regular mechanic, checking the shop's qualifications and track record, etc. (See the chapter titled, "Finding Mechanics You Can Trust" for more information on finding reputable repair shops.)

CHAPTER 6

Department Store Auto Centers

Many of the large department stores have automotive service departments that benefit from the name-recognition and large advertising budgets of the parent companies. The most common ones are Sears and Montgomery Ward; Macy's, Emporium, and Weinstock's also have automotive centers at some of their stores.

K-Mart also has automotive centers, but they have discontinued some of the services they used to offer. They no longer do tune-up work, but they still do oil changes, tires, brakes, exhaust systems, front end, air conditioning, and other minor repairs. The reason given for discontinuing tune-up work is that the parent company didn't want to invest the money that was required for up-to-date diagnostic equipment.

Department store auto centers are set up to do the "quick and easy" repairs, so they don't usually get into any major engine, drivetrain, or electrical problems. Most of their business is in tires and brakes, because they advertise heavily in those areas.

For routine maintenance and minor repairs, these auto

centers can offer high quality at low prices. Their mechanics are usually well trained in the areas of brakes and front end work; they use high-quality parts; and they usually offer service "packages" at low prices.

There are two major drawbacks of using department store service centers. The first one is their inability to diagnose difficult electrical and driveability problems. Their service centers are set up to do routine maintenance tune-ups, so their mechanics typically have little (if any) experience in diagnosing driveability problems on computer-controlled cars.

Sometimes their mechanics aren't even able to diagnose simple problems. I took my car to one of these service centers for new tires and overheard a conversation between another customer and one of their mechanics. The customer had bought one of their batteries that had suddenly gone dead. He told the mechanic that he had the battery checked at a service station and they said it had a dead cell, so it needed to be replaced. However, the mechanic said that he couldn't test the battery without charging it first (which is not necessarily true), so the customer would have to wait 30-45 minutes while it was being charged.

After about 45 minutes, the mechanic came back and told the customer that the battery was okay. When the customer asked, "What about the dead cell?", the mechanic said, "I don't care what that other shop said, the battery passed a load test, so there's nothing wrong with it."

There are actually three tests for a battery, and a battery that went dead should pass both a load test and a hydrometer test before someone says it's okay. That mechanic only did a load test (and he probably didn't do that right, either), so he sent that customer out on the road with a battery that would fail again.

The second drawback to using department store auto centers is the potential sale of unnecessary repairs. If their advertised prices are too low, they'll have to sell additional repairs to make a profit. Also, most (if not all) service writers and managers are paid a percentage of the sales, so they have a major incentive to sell a lot of additional repairs. In a lot of cases, the temptation to sell unnecessary repairs is too great. (After all, they are "mass merchandisers," set up to sell mass amounts of merchandise.)

Some of these service centers have a long history of selling unnecessary parts. They would run ads for tires and low-priced alignments, then they would try to sell a lot of ball joints, idler arms, shocks, and other suspension parts that weren't needed. People who came in for low-priced brake jobs were sold drums, rotors, calipers, master cylinders, and other unnecessary parts.

When I was working at an independent repair shop, we used to get a lot of calls from people who went to a well-known department store auto center for new tires and were told that they needed ball joints and other front end parts. To their credit, they called us to get a second opinion before they authorized any additional repairs.

In almost every case, we found that the repairs the auto center had recommended were not necessary. They were always trying to sell new ball joints, but 90-95% of the ones we checked weren't bad. When they tried to sell a major front end repair, we would occasionally find one bad part out of the 5 or 6 parts they were trying to sell. For example, if we were checking out a car that supposedly needed new ball joints, tie rod ends, and an idler arm, we might discover that the idler arm was bad, but all of the other parts were okay.

Undercover Investigations, 1990-92
Sears Auto Centers -- California, New Jersey, New York, Florida

On June 11, 1992 the California Department of Consumer Affairs announced that the state Bureau of Automotive Repair was seeking to revoke the repair licenses of all 72 Sears Auto Centers in the state, charging them with false or misleading statements, fraud, false advertising, and willful departure from accepted trade standards. The Consumer Affairs director stated, "These are not honest mistakes. This is the systematic looting of the public."

The charges against Sears were the result of a 15-month undercover investigation by the Bureau of Automotive Repair which started in December of 1990. After detecting a pattern of consumer complaints against Sears, the Bureau conducted 38 initial undercover runs at 27 of its repair shops, documenting the sale of unnecessary parts and services 90% of the time. The average bill for unnecessary repairs was $228; in some cases agents were charged as much as $550 for repairs that weren't needed.

The Bureau also claimed that in some cases, Sears employees used scare tactics to sell repairs, telling agents that certain brake parts were defective and unsafe, when they were in perfect working order. Agents said that Sears' mechanics made incompetent repairs--some cars were damaged, and one undercover car that went in for a brake inspection left the shop with no brakes.

After the initial investigation, Sears was notified of the results by the Bureau. The following month, undercover agents made 10 more visits to Sears' shops and documented the sale of unnecessary repairs 80% of the time. According to the Bureau, the number of items oversold was lower on the second round of visits.

Sears initial response to the charges was an angry denial of any wrongdoing, claiming that "the Bureau's undercover investigation was very seriously flawed..." and that the company would fight the charges in court. However, three days later, the New Jersey Division of Consumer Affairs announced that it had been conducting an (unrelated) undercover investigation of Sears Auto Centers and had documented the sale of unnecessary repairs during 12 visits to 6 Sears shops. Then the Florida Attorney General's office notified Sears that its repair shops were being investigated.

Due to the bad publicity, sales at Sears Auto Centers dropped 15-20%. Since the Auto Centers contribute about 9% of Sears' total revenue, the sales drop could have cost Sears $400-500 million over the course of a year. On June 22, the chairman of Sears admitted that "mistakes did occur" at shops in California and New Jersey, and promised to eliminate commissions and sales goals at the shops.

How did Sears get into so much trouble repairing cars? Simple--they had been advertising free brake inspections and brake jobs for $48-58 to bring in customers, and their service advisers were put on a commission/quota system that encouraged the sale of unnecessary repairs (especially the five items listed below). Employees who failed to meet their quotas were often disciplined by having their hours cut or being transferred to another department.

In September, a settlement was announced by Sears and the California Department of Consumer Affairs. Sears agreed to pay $8 million to settle the charges--$3 million for restitution, $3.5 million for costs of the investigation, and $1.5 million worth of tools and equipment for the state's community college system. Sears was allowed to continue operating repair shops in the state, but could face suspension if the shops violate the terms of the settlement during the next three years.

To settle the charges of selling unnecessary repairs in California and New Jersey, Sears agreed to offer restitution to any consumer nationwide who purchased a pair of brake calipers, a pair of coil springs, a pair of shock absorbers, a master cylinder, or an idler arm from August 1, 1990 to January 31, 1992. The company said that more than 900,000 consumers may be eligible. For those consumers who weren't satisfied with the coupon offer, Sears said it would honor its policy of "satisfaction guaranteed or your money back."

An investigation into Sears' auto repair practices by the New York Attorney General's office revealed problems far worse than those uncovered in California, including the widespread employment of service advisors with little or no previous training or experience in auto repair. In spite of their obvious lack of qualifications, their job description included inspecting and diagnosing vehicles prior to making service and repair recommendations to consumers.

At the Sears centers, the principal function of the service advisors was to generate sales of auto repair services and products. Their pay was based on an incentive compensation plan consisting of a minimal base salary plus commission that was tied directly to their total sales, so the more they sold, the more they were paid. In addition, the company ran contests to see who could produce the biggest increase in sales for specific parts or services.

The New York Attorney General claimed that unnecessary repairs were sold at Sears as a direct result of their "incentive compensation and goal-setting program," and that Sears service advisors often refused to honor lifetime service contracts they had sold for wheel alignments and other services, unless vehicle owners agreed to pay for additional repairs.

According to the Attorney General, the practices found at Sears were not limited to its auto centers in New York, but were being used nationwide, and by other companies as well. Following the investigations, Sears discontinued its sales incentive program, and put into place a number of safeguards to protect consumers. (See Chapter 19 for details.)

Undercover Investigations, 1983-85
Montgomery Ward Auto Centers, California

Over a three year period, district attorneys in two different counties filed separate consumer protection lawsuits against Montgomery Ward, Inc. for alleged unlawful and fraudulent business practices at its auto centers. The state Bureau of Automotive Repair had received numerous consumer complaints against the auto centers, so they conducted undercover investigations.

The first investigation was in Stanislaus County. When the investigation was completed, the district attorney filed suit against Montgomery Ward, claiming that its auto center was using unlawful business practices. They were accused of recommending unnecessary repairs, performing unnecessary or unworkmanlike repairs, misrepresenting the condition of parts on customers' vehicles, and damaging or sabotaging parts on customers' vehicles so that further repairs were required.

To settle the charges, Montgomery Ward paid $80,000 in fines and costs, and agreed to an injunction prohibiting all company employees in the state from any unlawful business practices (including those listed above).

About two years after the Stanislaus County case, another investigation of a Montgomery Ward Auto Center was done, this time in El Dorado County. The district attorney sued the parent company, claiming that it had used unlawful and fraudulent business practices. In the lawsuit, Montgomery Ward was accused of the following:

> "Representing to customers that specific work would be performed for a set price, when in truth and in fact upon completion of the specific work, a higher price was charged.
>
> Representing to customers that parts were damaged or needed to be replaced on automobiles when in truth and in fact, parts were not damaged or did not need to be replaced...
>
> Defendants made untrue and misleading statements to customers regarding necessary repairs and services...
>
> Defendants defrauded customers by representing to customers that parts needed to be replaced, which replacement was paid for by customers, when in fact the parts did not need to be replaced..."

The auto center was also accused of charging customers for repairs that had not been done. Some of the unnecessary repairs that they were accused of selling included tune-ups, alternators, voltage regulators, and master cylinders.

To settle the charges, Montgomery Ward paid $110,000 in fines and costs, and made restitution to 118 customers. The company also agreed to another injunction prohibiting all of its employees in the state from any unlawful business practices, including the allegations listed in the lawsuit.

Part of the settlement included an unusual condition; Montgomery Ward was required to pay the cost of constructing a mobile test bench which would be used by the Bureau to test the alternators, regulators, and master cylinders that the auto center had replaced. This was done to ensure that they were not replacing those parts unnecessarily.

This Montgomery Ward store was located in a small town (Placerville) and there was a lot of publicity surrounding the case after the district attorney filed the lawsuit. Shortly after the case was settled and the restitution was completed, the store closed.

Note: Montgomery Ward has made a number of changes in its compensation plans, among them the elimination of sales commission for mechanics in 1989. (See Chapter 19 for details.)

CHAPTER 7

Service Stations

As a general rule, many service stations are only interested in performing repairs that are "quick and easy." Few stations have enough room to do major repairs that could tie up a service stall (or parking space) for several days or weeks, so they usually turn away jobs that they think are difficult or will take a long time to complete. This is especially true in the areas of major engine and transmission repairs, electrical work, and computer problems.

Service station mechanics normally have to work on all types of vehicles, from domestics and imports to cars and trucks, which prevents them from becoming extremely knowledgeable concerning any one type. So, although they can usually diagnose and repair the "easy" problems on many different kinds of vehicles, they are normally unable to handle the "hard" ones. Many stations regularly refer their customers to dealerships or other shops for jobs that are too difficult for them.

Most service stations' weakest areas are their lack of training and skills concerning late-model cars, and their inability to handle difficult problems. (This is generally true of all types of shops, not just service stations.) Their strong points are in the areas of convenient locations, the acceptance of oil company credit cards for repair bills, and prices that are usually lower than independent repair shops and dealership service departments.

Service stations can sometimes be convenient and inexpensive places to get quality work done on routine repairs and maintenance. Some of the repairs they excel in are lube and oil changes, (maintenance) tune-ups, brakes, cooling systems, air conditioning, minor electrical problems, and front end work.

Make sure you choose a shop that only employs ASE certified technicians who receive continuous training to keep up with the latest technology. If your area has AAA Approved Auto Repair Facilities, choose a shop that is in that program. (See the chapter titled, "Finding Mechanics You Can Trust" for more information.)

"SUPERSTATIONS"

Some stations do have mechanics who are highly skilled and able to handle difficult problems, but they are definitely in the minority. These stations should be easy to spot--they'll usually have the latest equipment and a booming business, too. Since highly-skilled mechanics are hard to find, word travels fast when someone finds a mechanic who is able to diagnose and repair problems that other shops couldn't fix. I know of several "superstations" in my area that have sophisticated diagnostic equipment and employ 4-6 technicians who are highly skilled.

RIP-OFFS

Consumers have been ripped off in two ways by service stations in the past--from being sold unnecessary repairs due to incompetent diagnosis in some cases and fraud in others. Some stations only rip off an occasional customer while others make a serious effort to rip off as many people as possible. Many service station mechanics are paid a commission on the parts and labor they sell, a practice that encourages the sale of unnecessary repairs.

In what is a blatant example of auto repair fraud, some service stations located out of town on lonely stretches of highway have used scare tactics and sabotage to sell unnecessary repairs. While pretending to check the oil or tires, unscrupulous mechanics have cut fan belts, hoses, and tires; some have even squirted oil on shock absorbers so they would appear to be leaking.

After the sabotage is done, the customer is called over to look at the problem that was "discovered." The hook that is used to trap the victim is the statement that the vehicle is not safe to drive, that it will never make it to the next town. Since the average motorist does not want his car to break down on a deserted highway, he becomes a victim of a repair scam. To prevent this from happening to you, never leave your vehicle unattended when stopping for gas.

Undercover Investigation--
Service Stations in Arizona

According to the Arizona Attorney General's office, most of the auto repair fraud in that state occurs at service stations located out of town on the highways. These stations are independently owned and carry the names of most (if not all) of the major oil companies.

Unlucky motorists stopping for self-service gas have been sold unnecessary coil springs, shock absorbers, tires, fan clutches, alternators, and repairs on transmissions and differentials. Coil springs were the most common, because they are a fast, high-profit item, followed by shocks and tires.

The Attorney General's office had received numerous consumer complaints against a particular service station, which was located in a remote area on an interstate highway, so an undercover investigation was done. A female agent was wired to record the conversation, then she drove a motor home to the service station for gas.

A station employee came out and took a look at the tires on the motor home, then informed the agent that the tires should be replaced because they were damaged. (He said they were "coming apart or separating.") When the agent told him that the tires were new (they only had about 1,000 miles on them), he changed his story. He then told her that the tires were the wrong size and load rating for the motor home, and that they weren't safe to drive on. Naturally, the station happened to have the "proper" tires on hand.

At this point, the agent agreed to buy a new set of tires and requested that they put her old tires (the ones that only had 1,000 miles on them) in the back of the motor home. After leaving the station, she checked the tires they had put in the back and discovered that they were someone else's old tires, not the new ones that had been on the motor home. The agent went back and demanded that they return her tires, and they eventually did. (Apparently, the station had planned on keeping her tires to resell to someone else.)

Undercover Investigation--
Service Stations in Nevada

Due to budget restrictions, only one undercover investigation has been done in Washoe County, Nevada in the last ten years. As a result of that investigation, civil and criminal complaints were filed by the district attorney against one Mobil station and one Texaco station (both were in-dependently-owned), along with four other shops. Civil complaints were also filed against three additional shops. All of the shops were charged with selling unnecessary parts and/or repairs in the Reno area.

The district attorney's office had several undercover vehicles prepared by an automotive expert. The vehicles had all new suspension and brake parts which were marked so the investigators could tell which parts (if any) were replaced during repairs. To create a brake problem, bolts on the master cylinder were loosened, causing the brake light (in the dash) to come on. The bolts were so loose that anyone doing a quick visual inspection would notice, and tightening them was all that was necessary to cure the problem.

The vehicles were then taken to the stations for diag-nosis and repairs. Out-of-state license plates and female undercover agents were used so the shops would not sus-pect that they were subjects of an investigation.

At the Texaco station, the agent was told that a com-plete brake job was needed, even though the vehicle had all new brake parts. After the agent paid for the brake job, the vehicle was inspected to see what repairs had ac-tually been done. All of the original brake parts (which had been marked) were still on the car, so criminal and civil charges were filed against the mechanic and the shop for charging for repairs that had not been done. The me-chanic pleaded guilty to a criminal charge of "obtaining money by false pretenses" and was put on probation. The mechanic and shop owner paid civil fines to settle the charges.

At the Mobil station, the agent was sold a new master cylinder to cure the problem. Civil and criminal charges were filed, but the criminal charges were later dropped. The shop paid a fine to settle the civil charges.

As a result of unrelated undercover investigations in different states, numerous independently-owned service stations representing Chevron, Exxon, Mobil, Shell, Texaco, and Union 76 oil companies have been charged with similar fraudulent business practices.

In some cases, the oil companies have been asked by prosecutors why they allow the stations to stay in business. The standard reply seems to be, "They are independently-owned stations, and we have no control over how they are run." However, they do allow them to do business under the oil companies' names, providing them with free signs and other advertising. All they would have to do is remove the signs and company name, and most (if not all) of those stations would go out of business.

Note: To make sure you don't end up in a dishonest or incompetent service station, make sure you check their track record *before* taking your vehicle in for repairs. Always call your local Better Business Bureau to find out their complaint history, and ask other people in the area what kind of reputation the shop has.

CHAPTER 8

Muffler Shops

Before I describe how some muffler shops have cheated
consumers in the past, I should give some basic information about exhaust systems and exhaust repairs. If you
understand why (and when) it's sometimes necessary to
install additional parts with a new muffler, you should be
able to tell when someone is trying to sell you parts you
don't need.

Exhaust systems are located underneath the vehicle,
where they are "out of sight and out of mind." Because of
this, minor problems often go unnoticed until they develop into major ones. A leaking exhaust system can allow
carbon monoxide to enter the passenger compartment,
causing drowsiness, unconsciousness, or death. To prevent this from happening, the exhaust system should be
periodically inspected for leaks.

Geographical location, climate, and driving conditions
can determine the useful life of exhaust system components. Salt in the air and salt used on the roads accelerate
the corrosion and rusting of exhaust pipes and mufflers.
Because of this, the exhaust pipes and muffler may only
last two or three years on a vehicle in Florida compared to
eight or ten years on one in Arizona.

On virtually all new vehicles, the exhaust pipes are welded to the muffler. When a muffler is replaced, the pipes must be cut and reattached to the new muffler. There are two ways to connect the pipes to the new muffler--by welding or the use of muffler clamps.

It's not always possible to get a perfect seal when using clamps, so most muffler shops prefer to weld the pipes to the muffler. However, if the pipes are severely rusted, they can't be welded.

Rust on the outside of the pipe that is superficial (i.e., it can be wiped off or removed with rust remover, or it is confined to small dots on the outside) will not prevent a good weld from being made. However, rust that has given the outside of the pipe a lumpy or flaky brown texture, or has penetrated through the outer layer of the pipe, will prevent a good weld between the pipe and muffler. If this is the case, a new pipe will have to be installed with the muffler.

Sometimes an exhaust pipe becomes so rusty that you can poke a hole in it or break off pieces of it using pliers (or even your fingers). A pipe this rusty definitely needs to be replaced for two reasons--because it can't be welded to the muffler, and more importantly, because it's not safe to leave it on the vehicle.

RIP-OFFS

In the past, many muffler shops have used two different strategies to lure more customers to their shops and to extract more money from them once they were there. The first strategy is the use of deceptive advertising; the second is the sale of unnecessary parts and repair work.

Deceptive advertising means that a particular part or service is offered at an unusually-low price without any intention of actually delivering that part or service at that price to most of the people who come in to purchase it.

One type of deceptive advertising (known as "bait and switch") involves telling the customer that the special sale items are all sold out, then trying to sell them another higher-priced item instead. Many businesses have been caught using this scheme when it was discovered that they never had any of the sale items in the store, indicating that they never intended to sell any of them at the advertised price.

Another type of deceptive advertising, one that has been used extensively in the auto repair industry, involves requiring almost all customers to buy additional parts and/or labor along with the sale-priced item.

Undercover Investigations, 1986-89
Midas Muffler & Brake Shops, California

After numerous consumer complaints were received by the California Bureau of Automotive Repair, the Bureau and several district attorneys' offices investigated nine Midas Muffler & Brake Shops in northern California. All of the shops were individually-owned franchises, and were located in four counties. These shops, along with their parent company (Midas International), were charged by the state with alleged violations that included deceptive advertising and the sale of unnecessary parts and repairs.

One of the deputy district attorneys who worked on the case claimed that the muffler they had advertised for $18.95 did not exist. He said that an additional $6 charge for clamps, hangers, pipes, or welding was added to all $18.95 muffler jobs.

Advertisements for automotive service are required by law to disclose the likelihood of additional charges. The type used for this disclosure must be at least one-half the size of the type used for the advertised price.

The muffler ads used by those shops did offer some disclosure, but the wording and the type size did not comply with the law. The parent company quickly changed its advertising when it was contacted by the district attorney's office.

To settle the case out of court, Midas International agreed to pay a civil judgment of $100,000 and the individual shops agreed to pay an additional $400,000. A permanent injunction was entered against all Midas Muffler & Brake Shops in California prohibiting the sale of unnecessary parts and repairs, and advertising to install mufflers unless the advertised price includes all charges. (This settlement also involved brake and suspension repairs. See the chapter titled, "Brake Shops" for more details.)

Sometimes it is necessary to replace other parts when a new muffler is being installed. (This is especially true if the pipes are severely rusted.) However, many muffler shops routinely attempt to sell new pipes, hangers, clamps, and/or adapters to every customer that comes into their shop for a new muffler.

If your vehicle is in a muffler shop for exhaust work, hopefully you have already checked the shop out using the methods mentioned in this book, so you are sure that they can be trusted. If not, the best way to avoid being sold unnecessary parts and repairs is to wait at the shop while they do the work, and to insist that they show you what parts need to be replaced so you can make an informed decision.

A lot of people will ask the mechanic to show them (and explain to them) why a particular part needs to be replaced, then they pretend to understand and agree with the mechanic, even though they don't have any idea what he's talking about. (Why do people do this? Probably because they don't want to look stupid in front of the mechanic.)

Don't do this! If you don't understand what they are saying, admit it, then ask them to explain it to you in language that you can understand. Better yet, bring someone with you who knows something about cars.

Beware of shops that try to sell you a new catalytic converter when you only brought your vehicle in for a muffler or exhaust pipe. Converters rarely fail--when they do, the emissions reading at the tailpipe will be considerably higher, or the vehicle will experience a drastic loss of power (in some cases, the vehicle won't even run).

Muffler shops don't have the equipment or the training to diagnose a converter as the cause of higher emissions, and if your vehicle actually ran that bad because the converter had failed, you probably wouldn't be taking it to a muffler shop to get it checked out.

You may be told that your converter should be replaced because it's "rusted out," but rust on the outside is normal, as long as the metal casing is solid and there are no leaks. (This is also true for exhaust pipes and mufflers.) If they say the converter is leaking, ask them to show you the leak, then get a second opinion--and another estimate--before you allow them to replace it. (Yes, I know this is inconvenient, but so is paying $400 or more for a converter that you don't need. Also, converters are often covered by the manufacturer's 5 year/50,000 mile emissions warranty, so if yours really is bad, you may be able to have it replaced at no charge by a dealership.)

Unless you plan on keeping your vehicle forever, avoid high-priced "lifetime-guarantee" mufflers. If your original muffler lasted 70-80,000 miles, the rest of the vehicle might be ready for a trade-in (or the junkyard) long before a regular replacement muffler goes out again.

Beware of shops that try to charge you for adapters that they claim are necessary to install a new muffler. When they mention adapters, you'll know they're not installing the right muffler, but instead are trying to install one that's cheap and in-stock. All mufflers are not the same, and if the wrong one is installed, driveability and/or emissions problems may develop.

Before you give the OK for new exhaust pipes or other repairs, check the parts yourself using the guidelines in this chapter. If they don't look bad to you, but the mechanic claims they are, don't get into an argument with him. Just say that you can't have any more work done at that time and they will have to put your vehicle back together so you can drive it home. (Then you can take it to another shop for a second opinion.)

A difficult situation can arise if you are told that they can't put your vehicle back together unless they install the new parts that they have been trying to sell you. Details on what you can do if you find yourself in this predicament are given in the chapter titled, "Avoiding Rip-Offs."

Instead of going to different shops to get work done at the lowest prices, going to the trouble of taking your vehicle to another shop to get a second opinion, or wondering whether the additional repairs you bought were really needed, try to find a mechanic you can trust using the guidelines in this book. You will probably end up saving money in the long run because you won't be paying for a lot of unnecessary repairs.

If you have found a reputable repair shop with well-trained mechanics, but they don't do muffler work, ask them to recommend a good muffler shop. Most mechanics know which shops in their area can be trusted to do an honest, high-quality job.

CHAPTER 9

Dealership
Service Departments

Many vehicle owners will not use new car dealership service departments for two reasons--one, because they think that dealerships charge too much, and two, because they're not able to talk directly to the mechanic who will be working on their car.

The perception that dealerships charge too much is often a result of past experiences people have had combined with a comparison of prices charged by independents and dealerships. As a general rule, the posted hourly labor rates at most independent repair shops are lower than those at most dealership service departments. (When I was working at an independent, many of our customers told us that they preferred our shop over the local dealerships because our prices were lower.)

There are several reasons why dealerships often charge more than other shops. The first one is higher overhead; mechanics in dealerships are often paid more (and have more benefits) than mechanics working in other repair shops, and dealerships usually have a lot more expensive equipment that is required to work on newer models.

Another reason for dealership prices being higher is

that their service departments are not usually willing to give away any parts or labor on a job that turned out to be more difficult or expensive than originally estimated. Because each department's profitability is constantly monitored by upper management (and accountants), service personnel will usually do whatever it takes to make a profit on every job.

On the other hand, many independent shops will absorb the additional time that is required to finish a difficult job, and will sometimes even give away parts to avoid creating an unpleasant customer relations problem. (When things go wrong, as they often do in the auto repair business, most shops would rather lose money on a job than lose a good customer.)

Many independent shops don't even know how much they need to charge just to stay in business. Some of them have a vague idea, but they're afraid to charge that much for fear of losing customers. Because of this, a great number of independent shops are so unprofitable that they are inches away from going out of business. Many shops do go out of business; some survive by working long hours, employing lower-paid (i.e., less-skilled) mechanics, and not upgrading shop equipment.

The advantages of using a dealership service department (that sells your type of vehicle) include: expert knowledge of your vehicle (at least in theory), factory technical information and assistance, factory-trained mechanics (again, in theory), the use of original-equipment parts, and the availability of binding arbitration.

Binding arbitration (through Autocap) is usually available to resolve disputes between dealerships and consumers. There is usually no charge to consumers for this service, and it can save the time and expense of going to court. Decisions are binding on the dealership, but not on the consumer, who is free to take his case to court if he is not satisfied.

Dealership mechanics are *usually* specialists in one repair area of one brand of vehicles (for example, one mechanic might repair transmissions only, while another mechanic might only repair computer systems). Because they have access to factory training and technical assistance that is not usually available to mechanics working in independent shops, they are *usually* more knowledgeable concerning the types of vehicles they work on.

As stated earlier, one of the reasons that dealerships have higher overhead is that their mechanics are usually paid more than those working in other repair shops. Generally speaking, dealership mechanics are paid more because they have had more training and are more skilled in their particular area. (They have to be pretty sharp to repair new cars.)

While it is true that consumers are more likely to find highly-skilled technicians (for a particular vehicle) at a dealership, it's not true that *all* mechanics working in dealerships are highly skilled. There is a serious shortage of top-notch mechanics and dealerships are affected, too. I have met quite a few dealership mechanics who are highly-skilled, but I have also seen many who were fairly incompetent.

In the past, I've had to repair many vehicles that were misdiagnosed or "hacked over" by dealership mechanics. Some good examples of this involved mechanics who replaced 6 or 8 computer parts on a vehicle before the problem was fixed. (Although it's sometimes necessary to replace 2 or 3 parts to repair a computer system, the only situation that would justify replacing that many parts would be if the engine caught on fire and all those parts were burned.)

Even though a dealership's posted labor rate may be higher than the labor rate at other repair shops, a dealership can still perform some types of repairs for less money. This is especially true of repairs on computer systems and other "high-tech" items on late-model vehicles. A factory-trained specialist should be able to diagnose and repair difficult problems much faster than a mechanic who works on several (or many) different types of vehicles.

Sometimes a mechanic has to make an educated guess concerning which part to replace. This is where a dealership mechanic has a distinct advantage over an independent--he can usually borrow a new part from the parts department to see if that will cure the problem, and if it doesn't, he can usually return it so the customer won't have to pay for it.

Independent shops can't borrow parts. Once a part is installed, they have to keep it, which means that the customer will have to pay for it even if it didn't cure the problem. This can sometimes result in consumers paying more for repairs at an independent shop than they would have paid at a dealership.

If a particular problem is common to one model, the manufacturer may repair it for free, even though the official written warranty has expired. (This is known as a "secret warranty.") For example, I have seen Toyota dealerships replace some exhaust manifolds on vehicles with 100,000 miles on them, at no charge to the customer. These types of repairs are not widely known outside of dealerships, so customers may end up paying for repairs at independent shops that could have been done for free. (For more information, see the chapter titled, "Secret Warranties.")

Even though dealerships have factory training and other advantages, they still have trouble finding and keeping good mechanics just like any other business. Sometimes new mechanics just don't work out, and a bad one can mess up a lot of cars before he is fired. One local dealer-ship couldn't perform any smog inspections for a while because it didn't have any mechanics who could pass the new state test for a smog license.

The disadvantages of using a dealership service de-partment (that sells your type of vehicle) include: repair bills that are often higher than independent shops for the same repair, not being able to talk to the person who is going to work on your vehicle, and sometimes encounter-ing an indifferent attitude concerning the cost of repairs and whether they will be completed on time.

Posted Labor Rates vs. Actual Labor Rates

One of the things to watch out for at dealership service departments is when their posted labor rate is lower than their actual labor rate (based on actual time spent on the job). For example, an independent repair shop that has a posted labor rate of $50 per hour may charge $75 labor for a front brake job, because the job takes 1.5 hours. However, a dealership with a posted labor rate of $50 per hour may charge $100 labor for the same job, making their actual labor rate $66 per hour, because it's still only a 1.5 hour job.

This is a fairly common practice, resulting in so many complaints that dealerships in some states are now re-quired to post a notice explaining that their labor charges are based on "established times" for particular repairs and may be higher than the posted labor rates for the actual time spent working on a vehicle.

When this method of pricing is used, consumers are not able to make accurate price comparisons based on the posted labor rates. If you call a dealership (or any other shop) to compare prices, make sure you get the total labor charges for a particular repair, as well as a breakdown of the parts to be changed (and their prices) so you can tell what the actual labor rates are.

Charging for Warranty Work

Another thing to watch out for at dealership service departments is the practice of charging for diagnosis and/or repairs that should be covered under the warranty. One way this is done is when consumers bring their vehicles in for repairs without knowing that they are covered under the warranty, and the service personnel fail to mention it, so the vehicle owners end up paying for the repairs.

The other way this is done is when consumers expect the repairs to be done under the warranty, but they are given a phony story explaining why the repairs aren't covered or why they'll have to pay for diagnosis. (If a dealership tries to pull this scam on you, ask to speak to the service manager, and if he doesn't resolve the problem to your satisfaction, call the manufacturer's customer service number for assistance.) The following true story of a dealership that tried to pull this scam on me illustrates how this is done.

When my car was about three years old, I took it to a local dealership to have some repairs done that were covered by the 5 year/50,000 mile emissions warranty. The service writer told me that I would have to pay $50 (for 1 hour of labor) to diagnose the problem, then if it turned out that the problem was covered by the warranty, the actual repairs would be free, but I would still have to pay the $50 charge for diagnosis.

At this point, I told the service writer that I had worked in several dealerships as a mechanic, and none of them had charged for diagnosis of problems that were covered under warranty. As soon as he heard that, he said, "Well, if it turns out that the problem is covered by the warranty, you won't be charged for the diagnostic time." When I picked up my car at the end of the day, the diagnostic charge had been crossed off and the repairs were done under the warranty.

That service writer insisted on charging me for diagnosing the problem, even though it was covered by the warranty. (Fortunately, I knew better, otherwise I would have paid the $50.) I don't believe it was just an honest mistake, because he had worked there for about 8 years and seemed to be fairly knowledgeable concerning late-model cars.

Why would a dealership try to charge customers for repairs that could be done under warranty? Because they make more money per hour on cash customers than they do on warranty work. The car manufacturers decide how much per hour they will pay for warranty work, and they also set limits on how much labor time they will pay for each repair.

For example, a dealership may only receive $42 per hour for warranty work, but charge $50 per hour for cash customers. A manufacturer may only pay for one-half hour of diagnostic time for a particular problem under warranty, but a dealership could charge a cash customer one hour (or more) to diagnose the same problem.

As you can see, dealerships have a major financial incentive to charge customers for repairs that should be done under warranty, so it's wise to question or challenge them if they try to charge you for something that you think should be done for free. If all else fails, call the manufacturer's customer service number for assistance before paying for diagnosis or repairs.

Selling Undercoating on New Vehicles

Several state attorneys general have mentioned recent instances of new car dealers selling undercoating services to buyers of new vehicles. One dealer in Missouri has been charged with selling unnecessary undercoating, and other states are looking into the practice also.

In the past, undercoating was a useful service because it protected metal parts that were susceptible to corrosion. However, most new vehicles today use plastic or corrosion-resistant metal for the undersides, so undercoating is not usually necessary.

If a dealer tries to sell you this service, tell him you want to check with the manufacturer first, then call their customer service number and ask if undercoating is necessary on that particular vehicle.

Charging for Unnecessary Maintenance

A practice at dealership service departments that is not as common as the first two involves charging for scheduled maintenance that the manufacturers say does not need to be done for another 15-30,000 miles (or more). The following stories of two dealerships that were accused of doing that illustrate some of the practices consumers should guard against.

Undercover Investigation, 1989-90
Lodi Honda, California

After receiving a consumer complaint against a Honda car dealership in Lodi, California, the Bureau of Automotive Repair and the San Joaquin County district attorney's office conducted an undercover investigation. When the investigation was completed, the district attorney's office filed a consumer protection lawsuit against Lodi Honda, an independently-owned new car dealership, asking for civil penalties of $1 million.

Lodi Honda was accused of charging over 2,000 customers for service that was either unnecessary or never done. According to the Bureau, undercover agents took several Hondas to the dealership, requesting that 30,000 mile services be performed. The Bureau's report claimed that Lodi Honda personnel performed service that was not recommended by Honda Motor Corp. until 45,000 and 60,000 miles. The report also claimed that those services were not explained to investigators until after they had been done. Bureau officials claimed that they inspected a vehicle after the service appointment and found that some services listed as being completed were not done.

The Bureau's report concluded: "This constitutes fraud, false and misleading statements, and false and misleading documents. It is apparent that Lodi Honda is engaging in unethical and unfair business practices, in that they are charging for services and receiving higher profits at the expense of the consumer."

The owner of Lodi Honda agreed to pay a total of $170,000 to settle the charges. ($20,000 for civil penalties, $35,000 for investigative and legal costs, $115,000 for restitution)

Undercover Investigation, 1989-90
Gene Gabbard Honda, California

In a similar case, the owner of Gene Gabbard Honda in Stockton was sued by the District Attorney's office in 1990 over the alleged sale of unnecessary parts while performing 15,000, 30,000, and 45,000 mile services. The Bureau said the undercover vehicles they sent in for service already had new spark plugs, distributor rotors, and fuel filters, but they were replaced anyway. The alleged overcharges varied from $40-60 for approximately 400 customers. To settle the charges, the dealership agreed to pay a total of $61,000 which included more than $21,000 in restitution.

To guard against this practice, consumers should check their owners' manuals to verify that the recommended services are actually required to keep up the warranty.

Most tune-up parts, including spark plugs, are covered under the emission warranty for the first 30,000 miles (or whenever the manufacturer recommends the first scheduled replacement).

Emission control and computer system parts are covered under warranty for 5 years or 50,000 miles on pre-1990 cars and light/medium duty trucks. For 1990 and newer models, all emission control and computer system parts are covered under warranty for 3 years or 50,000 miles; the repair or replacement of some high-priced defective parts listed in the owner's manual may be covered up to 7 years or 70,000 miles.

Note: For complete information on emission warranties, contact the Environmental Protection Agency (see Chapter 15), or your vehicle manufacturer.

CHAPTER 10

Lube & Oil Shops

Shops that specialize in fast and inexpensive "lube & oil" changes have become very popular in recent years. The convenience and low prices of these shops can be very appealing, but problems and abuses have occurred at some of them in the past, so consumers should exercise caution when using these shops.

There are two basic types of lube and oil shops. One type only does maintenance work such as lubrication, oil changes, and filters; the other type does tune-ups, smog inspections, and other repairs in addition to lube and oil changes.

This chapter will cover shops that only perform maintenance work. For information on shops that do tune-ups, smog inspections, and other repairs in addition to lube and oil changes, see the chapter titled, "Tune-up Shops."

Lube and oil shops are almost always franchises, which means that a parent company lends its name and sets up the business for someone who is willing to pay a franchise fee. A background in service (or repair) of motor vehicles is usually not required, so many franchisees have little or no experience in this area. While it is true that performing lube and oil changes does not require a great amount of skill or education, and the parent company usually provides some training for the new owner, the lack of automotive experience can sometimes cause problems.

Since these shops are performing this service for a price that is usually much lower than that charged by repair shops, many of them are forced to hire inexperienced workers who will settle for low wages. This is where the danger lies--many of the employees doing the lube and oil changes have no prior experience in servicing motor vehicles.

Workers are often under pressure to sell additional filters and other services while still completing the lube and oil change in 10-15 minutes, a situation that often results in mistakes being made when the worker has to choose between doing the job well and doing it quickly. To save time, some workers have installed incorrect oil filters because they did not have the correct one in stock. Oil drain plugs that did not tighten properly were not repaired because it would have taken too long.

A good example of what can go wrong during a lube and oil change occurred in several shops that were part of a well-known California chain. (At least one of them was a company-owned shop, so the problem wasn't limited to just a few franchisees.) They had been advertising heavily, promoting a low-priced lube, oil, and filter service.

Some of the vehicles that they had serviced experienced engine damage so severe that the engines had to be completely rebuilt. Shop personnel had returned several vehicles to customers with no oil in them, and the customers drove several blocks before noticing that something was seriously wrong. Unfortunately, by that time, the engines were already ruined.

The engines in several other vehicles were damaged when all of the oil suddenly leaked out due to improper oil filter installation. Some of their workers had not removed the old oil filter gaskets from the engines before installing new filters, so it was just a matter of time before major leaks developed.

Even though it was the shops' negligence that caused the engine damage, they didn't pay the entire cost of the overhauls--they pro-rated the customers' share of the bills based on vehicle mileage. Those customers ended up paying hundreds of dollars (in some cases, over a thousand) for an engine overhaul after bringing their vehicle in for a simple, "inexpensive" oil change.

Some of the mistakes made by inexperienced personnel at lube and oil shops include improper installation of oil filters, failure to repair leaking oil drain plugs, use of incorrect fluids and filters, and failure to put the proper amount of oil in the engine (all of which can cause serious engine damage). Since a typical lube and oil shop needs to service about 35 vehicles per day to be profitable, mistakes such as these are not that unusual.

Avoid using these shops for anything other than lube and oil changes. Some of them have started to service automatic transmissions, which has created some expensive problems. The workers in lube and oil shops generally have no experience or knowledge of automatic transmissions, so they wouldn't be able to perform any of the inspections or adjustments that should be done when a transmission is serviced.

During a one-year period, a transmission mechanic that I know had to repair several automatic transmissions that had been serviced by a local lube and oil shop. They failed to tighten all of the filter screws inside the transmission, and some of the screws fell out. Those loose screws caused the gears to jam, resulting in cracked transmission cases. In order to repair those transmissions, they had to be rebuilt with new cases (at a cost of $800-$1,000).

Another problem area is the use of inexpensive, low-quality parts. Although virtually all lube and oil shops use name-brand motor oil, not all use high-quality, name-brand oil filters and air filters. Using inexpensive filters, *especially oil filters*, is risky because many of them do not filter out as many particles as the name-brand ones do. Trying to save a dollar or two on a filter can result in increased engine wear and premature engine failure. *Insist on high-quality, name-brand parts.*

Putting the wrong fluid in a vehicle is another potential problem area for these shops. Due to the high-volume business that is done by most of them, fluids are usually bought and stored in bulk quantities. Hose reels are used to dispense most fluids. If the hoses containing different fluids all look the same, the wrong fluid may be put in your vehicle by an inexperienced or distracted worker. Many shops have color-coded hoses to prevent this from happening. Make sure the hoses used for dispensing fluids are clearly marked.

Brake fluid should not be stored and dispensed out of large barrels or other containers because the fluid will absorb moisture from the air and become contaminated. The use of contaminated brake fluid will cause rust or corrosion to form inside the brake cylinders and calipers, resulting in premature brake failure. Make sure the brake fluid is stored and dispensed out of small containers (one gallon or less).

Lube & Oil Guidelines

Lube and oil shops can be a convenient and inexpensive resource for servicing your vehicle--if some guidelines are followed. Some shops use high-quality, name-brand parts and are professionally run, but since almost all of these shops are franchises with different owners, even those under the same name may not provide the same level of service. If you should decide to use a lube and oil shop instead of a regular repair shop, these guidelines should be followed:

1. Make sure they use high-quality, name-brand parts.
2. Ask how much experience the workers have--if they just started working there, ask for someone with more experience. (Don't go to a brand-new lube and oil shop until they've been open for several weeks. When a new one first opens for business, most of the work ers will usually be new and inexperienced. Let them learn on someone else's vehicle.)
3. Beware of shops that try to sell air filters, breather elements, or other items every time the oil is changed. Depending on driving conditions, those items normally last at least 10-15,000 miles.
4. Don't use these shops for automatic transmission services.
5. Look for a clean, well-organized shop--chances are that if they are conscientious with their workplace, they will be with your vehicle, too. Make sure all fluid-dispensing hoses are clearly marked to prevent mistakes.
6. Avoid shops that look like a "three-ring circus"-- hectic, frazzled workers are more likely to make mistakes than calm, orderly ones.

CHAPTER 11

Undercover Investigations

Note: Most of the shops that are mentioned as subjects of undercover investigations and disciplinary actions are individually-owned franchises of well-known chains. This means that the parent companies do not have total control over how the individual shops are run, which explains why some shops belonging to a chain were charged with unlawful and/or fraudulent business practices while others were not.

It would be unfair (and inaccurate) to suggest that *all* of the shops belonging to those chains were charged with unlawful business practices, or were using the same tactics, and that is not my intention.

In most states, the Department of Consumer Affairs is responsible for overseeing the auto repair shops, as well as most other types of businesses that sell goods or services to consumers. In California and Michigan, there are separate agencies (the Bureau of Automotive Repair and the Bureau of Automotive Regulation, respectively) that license, regulate, and investigate auto repair shops.

Few states do undercover work on a regular basis (like California does). When asked why they don't, some of them said because they don't have the money or the manpower; others said it was because they don't have that much repair fraud in their state.

In talking with investigators who have done a lot of undercover work, I told them about the other states that claimed they didn't have that much fraud. The investigators thought that was unbelievable. Several of them commented that all those states had to do was make a few undercover runs at fifteen or twenty shops that advertised low-priced repairs, and they would quickly find out how much of a problem they really had.

Channel 2 TV in Michigan did a special on auto repair in October of 1989 that seemed to establish the truth of what those investigators had said. The station sent a reporter (with a hidden microphone) to twelve shops that advertised low-priced repairs; four of the twelve shops allegedly recommended unnecessary repairs. (For more details, see the story in the Tire & Alignment chapter.)

According to an investigator at the California Bureau, the reason that many of the other states don't think that auto repair fraud is very common is that they're using the number of consumer complaints to gauge the severity of the problem. He said that fewer than one out of a hundred people will file a complaint when they think they've been ripped off, so the problem is not that obvious until at least three or four complaints have been filed (which probably means that at least three or four hundred people were victimized). A good example of this is the Quality Tune-Up case, which the Bureau claimed involved about 70,000 alleged victims. In that case, the Bureau had only received about 125 consumer complaints.

The California Bureau (or BAR) is the most advanced and aggressive agency in the country for regulating and investigating auto repair shops. Because of this, local and state prosecuting attorneys have asked for their assistance in doing undercover investigations. They have also shared their expertise with investigators and attorneys in other states. Since they are recognized experts in their field, and their undercover methods are used elsewhere, I will briefly explain how they conduct investigations.

The majority of complaints, investigations, and disciplinary actions are against a small percentage of the repair shops in California. *Approximately 65% of all repair shops in the state received no formal complaints.* A small minority (7%) of the registered shops was responsible for nearly half of all formal complaints received by the BAR.

If the Bureau receives a lot of complaints against a shop, it will usually start an investigation. The most common complaints that trigger investigations are from customers who were sold hundreds of dollars worth of additional repairs after going to a shop that advertised low-priced tune-ups, brake jobs, mufflers, etc. Many of the complaints against those shops were also for repairs that were done in an incompetent manner.

When the BAR decides to conduct an investigation, it sends undercover vehicles to a shop to verify the routine sale of unnecessary repairs, using deceptive advertising ("bait & switch"), or any other unlawful and/or fraudulent business practice.

At the Bureau's laboratory, technicians prepare undercover vehicles that will be used to document fraudulent repair schemes. If their target is a tune-up shop, they may install old spark plugs in a vehicle and then replace all other tune-up parts with new ones. The new parts are then treated so it's not obvious that they were just installed. (This is usually done by making them look as dusty or dirty as the other parts on the vehicle.)

If their target is a brake shop, BAR technicians may replace all of the brake parts with new ones on some undercover vehicles, while on others they may replace everything but the brake shoes. For a transmission shop, technicians may install a completely rebuilt transmission that has an obvious minor, external problem (for example, a disconnected vacuum hose or misadjusted linkage). Most of the new parts are treated to look as dusty or dirty as other parts on the vehicle.

To document a case against a shop suspected of charging for repairs or services that were not done, BAR technicians put hidden seals on parts that will be broken if the repairs are actually done. The vehicle is then taken to the shop, where an undercover agent requests a particular repair or service. Immediately after the agent is charged for the repair, the vehicle is taken back to the BAR laboratory where the seal is examined to determine whether the repair was done or not.

After the vehicles are prepared for an undercover operation, BAR agents (posing as customers) take them to the suspect shops for diagnosis and repair. Most of the cases involve shops that advertise low-priced repairs, so the agents take the vehicles in for the advertised "specials" to see if the shops try to sell them unnecessary repairs.

According to the BAR, undercover vehicles that had all new tune-up parts (except for the spark plugs) were taken to well-known tune-up shops for their advertised $30-40 tune-ups. Undercover agents claim that those shops routinely replaced spark plug wires, rotors, distributor caps, filters, and PCV valves that had fewer than 50 miles on them, resulting in major tune-up work costing $100-200.

When brake shops were being investigated, BAR agents took undercover vehicles to well-known shops that advertised free inspections and $59 brake jobs. The agents claimed that the shops routinely replaced wheel cylinders, master cylinders, drums, rotors, and other brake items that only had a few miles on them. Instead of $59 brake jobs, agents were sold major brake work costing $300-500, most of which the BAR claims was unnecessary. The Bureau also claimed that scare tactics were used to sell additional repairs.

To document a case against a shop for selling unnecessary repairs (or charging for repairs that weren't done), at least three or four undercover cars are usually sent to that shop. By this time, the BAR usually has dozens of complaints from consumers regarding the same shop.

Sometimes statements from former employees are taken which indicate a plan to use "bait and switch" tactics, high-pressure sales (including the use of scare tactics), and the sale of unnecessary repairs. With the evidence from the undercover work, dozens of complaints from consumers, and statements from ex-employees, the Bureau is now ready to take action against a shop.

The BAR has three different ways to discipline repair shops--administrative action, civil action, and criminal action. Sometimes more than one action is taken against a shop. For example, if the Bureau wants to suspend or revoke a shop's repair license in addition to making the shop pay a large fine (or restitution), it will initiate both administrative and civil actions.

Administrative Action

Administrative actions are the most common form of discipline used by the BAR. The state attorney general, representing the Bureau, presents its case before an administrative law judge, who renders a decision regarding the shop's repair license.

For minor violations, suspension or revocation of a shop's repair license is usually stayed and the shop put on probation for one or two years. For more serious violations, a shop's license may be suspended for 3-30 days (during which the shop cannot perform any repairs). The shop may also be required to post a sign explaining why its repair license is suspended, and it will usually be put on probation for two to three years.

If the violations are very serious (for example, fraud or continued violations after previous disciplinary actions), a shop's license may be permanently revoked.

Civil Action

The Bureau can also initiate a civil action (lawsuit), brought by a government agency representing the public. This is usually done by the state attorney general or a county district attorney, and can result in fines, restitution, and/or court orders to discontinue certain business practices. Civil actions initiated by the Bureau are almost as common as administrative actions.

Criminal Action

The third disciplinary option available to the Bureau is a criminal action, usually brought by a city or county district attorney, resulting in a criminal conviction for violating the Automotive Repair Act or the Penal Code. Conviction can result in probation, imprisonment, fines, and/or restitution.

Shop owners have been sentenced to jail for 1-360 days for performing repairs while not registered or licensed, failing to give proper written estimates, doing repairs without proper authorization, falsely certifying emission control systems, and other violations.

Before the BAR decides on which course of action to take against a shop, it must consider the expense and effort required to win the case, the likelihood of winning, and which action will most benefit the public. If a shop repeatedly ignores warnings and violates probation from a previous disciplinary action, the Bureau will usually initiate an administrative action to permanently revoke the shop's repair license.

In cases that the BAR claims are obvious examples of unnecessary repair schemes, the Bureau will initiate a civil suit if they think the shop owner (or parent company) has enough money to pay a fine and make restitution. This is especially true in cases against large, well-known shops or chains--instead of revoking their licenses and closing them down (which would not help the people who paid for unnecessary repairs), the shops are usually allowed to stay in business if they stop the illegal practices, pay large fines, and make restitution.

To avoid criminal convictions or civil judgments that could ruin their businesses, and expose them to lawsuits from hundreds (or thousands) of customers, almost all shops agree to settle out of court. When this is done, the shop owner usually agrees to pay fines, restitution, and/or investigative expenses *without admitting any wrongdoing*. Because of this, there are practically no guilty pleas or convictions in any of the cases involving major undercover operations.

Subjects of Undercover Investigations

The following well-known chains have had one or more of their shops charged with unlawful and/or fraudulent business practices following undercover investigations between 1980 and 1994. Except as noted, the shop owners all agreed to out-of-court settlements without admission of wrongdoing. Significant totals of fines, penalties, restitution, and/or investigative costs paid by particular shops are also listed. The most recent ones are detailed in the appropriate chapters.

133

Aamco Transmissions[1] $600,000+
Avellino Tire & Auto Service Centers
Belle Tire Centers
Big O Tires[2] $169,000
Cottman Transmissions $60,000+
Econo Lube N' Tune[3]
Firestone Tire Centers $270,000
Gibraltar Transmissions[4]
Goodyear Tire Centers[5]
Grand Auto, Inc.
Interstate Transmissions
K Mart Corporation $50,000
Lee Myles Transmissions $52,500+
Midas Muffler & Brake Shops $500,000+
Montgomery Ward Auto Centers $190,000
Mr. Transmission
Pep Boys Manny Moe & Jack $65,000
Quality Tune-Up $2,000,000
Sears Auto Centers[6] $15,000,000+
Winston Tire Co.[7] $1,500,000

Notes -- [1]One shop admitted that its repair license was subject to discipline for committing a fraudulent act and making false or misleading statements.
[2]One shop admitted to making untrue or misleading statements, and fraudulently charging customers for repairs not done.
[3]Case pending, (owner left the state).
[4]One shop's repair license permanently invalidated for charges of fraud and making false or misleading statements.
[5]One shop admitted that its repair license was subject to discipline for recommending replacement of brake parts unnecessarily.

[6]California fine, investigative costs, & restitution $8 million; nationwide restitution program for 900,000 consumers estimated at an additional $7 million (plus).
[7]All company-owned stores, not franchises.

What Auto Mechanics Don't Want You to Know

CHAPTER 12

Avoiding Rip-offs;
Getting Your Money Back

The best way to avoid rip-offs is to use the guidelines in this book to locate a reputable shop that employs well-trained, highly-skilled technicians. However, that may not always be possible, so the following information is provided to help consumers avoid having to pay for unnecessary repairs.

If you are forced to take your vehicle to an unfamiliar shop, or if you just haven't found a reputable shop yet, be suspicious if they use scare tactics or pressure to sell you expensive additional repairs. Honest shops don't use scare tactics or pressure. All of the honest shops that I have run across have the same attitude--they just tell customers what is needed, and if they don't want to have it done, then that's okay with them.

Use common sense to determine whether repairs are urgently needed or not. *Don't be taken in by scare tactics!* If you weren't experiencing any problems before you brought your vehicle to the shop, it probably wouldn't hurt to put off any major repairs for a few more days (while you get a second opinion). Obviously, if they show you something like a cracked brake hose or a brake fluid leak, then you may need to have those items repaired immediately for safety reasons.

Before you give your approval for additional parts or repairs, check the parts yourself using the guidelines listed in the other chapters. If they don't look bad to you, but the mechanic claims they are, don't get into an argument with him. Just say that you can't have any more work done at that time and they will have to put your vehicle back together so you can drive it home. (Then you can take it to another shop for a second opinion.)

The following procedure can be used to protect yourself (and get your money back) if your vehicle is disabled at an unfamiliar shop, and you think they are trying to sell you unnecessary repairs.

A difficult situation can arise if you are told that they can't put your vehicle back together unless they install the new parts that they have been trying to sell you. When this happens, you have four choices--demanding (or simply threatening) to speak to the manager, threatening to call the state consumer protection agency and the Better Business Bureau to file complaints, having your vehicle towed to another shop, or paying for the additional repairs.

If you can't convince the manager to put your vehicle back together without the new parts, and you don't want to have your vehicle towed to another shop, tell them to go ahead with the additional repairs. *Make sure they put all of your old parts in the trunk, then pay for the repairs with a credit card*--don't pay with cash or a check.

You may be told that you can't have your old parts back because you were sold rebuilt ones at "exchange" prices, but this is only true if you don't pay the "core charge" on the parts. Pay the extra charge, if necessary, so you can have your old parts back. (The law states that repair shops must return old parts to consumers when requested, so don't let them tell you that you can't have them back.)

Without your old parts, you won't be able to prove that you were sold unnecessary repairs. After the dispute is settled (or if you discover that the repairs really were necessary), you can return the parts for a refund of the core charge.

Take your old parts to a reputable repair shop (a new car dealership that sells the same make of car would be ideal), then ask them if the parts look like they came from your car and whether they needed to be replaced. There may be a small charge for this, but it's worth it for your peace of mind; also, if it turns out that replacement wasn't necessary, another shop's statement will be helpful in getting your money back. *Get their statements in writing.*

If several mechanics tell you that it wasn't necessary to replace those parts, or worse yet, that the parts the shop supposedly replaced didn't come from your car, call the shop and ask to speak to the owner or manager. Tell him that you had the old parts checked out, that you were told they didn't need to be replaced, and you want your money back.

If the manager refuses to refund your money, tell him that you are going to notify the credit card company that you have a dispute with the shop and that you refuse to pay for that charge until the dispute is settled. (Before you do this, read the section on your credit card statement that explains your rights and restrictions. This is usually permitted for purchases over $50 that are made in your home state or within 100 miles of your mailing address. These restrictions may not apply if the credit card issuer owns or operates the repair shop.)

Then go home and write a letter to the shop owner or manager, repeating your demand for a refund, as well as the reasons why you think you are entitled to one. Be sure to make several copies of this "demand letter," then send it by registered mail to prove that it was received.

It's very important to follow these instructions carefully. The old parts, the statements from other mechanics, and the demand letter are all needed to refuse payment on your credit card or take the shop to court, so make sure they are done in the proper order. (Note: I don't recommend writing a check to the repair shop and then stopping payment on it. In some states it is against the law to write a check that bounces, and you may be subject to fines and/or imprisonment if you do this.)

Don't tell the shop that you intend to refuse payment on your credit card until *after* you have picked up your car and had the old parts checked by another shop. If they know ahead of time that you are going to refuse payment, they may insist that you pay cash before they let you pick up your car. If this happens, you may never get your money back, even if you take them to court and win--it's not easy to collect on a judgment if they don't feel like paying you.

When you refuse to pay for a particular charge on your credit card statement because of a dispute with a merchant, the credit card company does a "charge back" against that shop's account for the disputed amount. This must be done *before* you pay the disputed amount on your credit card statement.

Make sure you've had the old parts checked and sent the "demand letter" before payment is due on your credit card. If you haven't done both of those things yet, you may have to make a minimum payment on the disputed amount, but *don't pay the entire amount*.

After you have verified that the old parts didn't need to be replaced and sent the demand letter, notify the card company (in writing) that you have a dispute with the shop and that you refuse to pay that charge.

If you do refuse payment on your credit card account,

the shop may take you to court, especially if they think you have no grounds for a refund. However, if the shop has sold you unnecessary repairs and you've followed the above procedure, the shop owner will know he's going to lose, so he probably won't sue. Even if the shop doesn't file suit, the vehicle owner may choose to sue the shop in small claims court to resolve the dispute and to make it a public record.

Many repair shops (for example, all AAA Approved Repair Facilities and most new car dealership service departments) have arbitration procedures in place that can eliminate the need for expensive and time-consuming court cases. Decisions are usually binding on the shop only, giving the consumer the right to take his case to court if he doesn't think the decision was fair. Be sure to ask if this service is available.

IMPORTANT NOTE--

Using a credit card to avoid paying for unnecessary repairs is only effective on fairly simple repairs such as brakes, minor tune-ups, and front end work, because it's easy to verify whether the parts needed to be replaced. If you go to low-priced shops in spite of what you have learned in this book, it would be a good idea to protect yourself using a credit card. However, it's not easy (or cost-effective) to test carburetors, computers, or other electrical parts after they have been removed from the vehicle, so this procedure won't usually work on complex repairs.

CHAPTER 13

Secret Warranties:
How to Get Free Repairs

Almost all automotive warranties have a time and/or mileage limit, but they are not carved in stone. It is often possible to have repairs done at no charge, or at a greatly reduced charge, even though the written warranty has expired.

A shop owner or service manager may decide to repair a vehicle for free even though the warranty has expired if the vehicle owner is thought of as a valued, long-time customer. When a shop owner or manager gives a phony excuse such as, "Believe me, I really wish I could repair it for free, but the parts are only guaranteed for ninety days, so there's nothing I can do," what he's really saying is that he doesn't see that person as a customer who's valued enough to bend the rules a little, so he's trying to brush him off.

So how can you be thought of as a "valued customer"? By having most (or all) of your repair work done at one shop, so they recognize your name. It also helps to recommend the shop to others--and make sure they mention your name when they bring their vehicle to the shop for the first time. (Obviously, you won't be seen as a valued customer if you always take your vehicle to different shops, trying to get the lowest price.)

> Note: The following information about warranties
> on automotive parts has been a well-kept secret. For
> years, shop owners and service managers have hid-
> den behind the "official" warrranty to avoid doing re-
> pairs over again. It's time to even the odds a little by
> letting consumers know that it's just an excuse.

Technically, most parts do have a specific warranty period, but this is also negotiable between the repair shop and
its supplier. The "valued customer" theory applies to repair shops and their suppliers, too, so if a shop does a fair
amount of business with a parts supplier, they should be
able to return parts that went bad within a reasonable time
period after the normal warranty runs out.

How far out of the normal warranty period the vehicle
can be and still be repaired for free depends on how valued the customer is, as well as how much it's going to
cost the shop. (This applies to the shop/supplier relation-
ship, too.)

In most cases, a shop can return a defective part and
get a free replacement even if it's been six or eight months
(or more), so the most they would lose is the labor charge.
It's usually a lot easier to negotiate a free repair if it
doesn't require a lot of labor to replace the part. If a significant amount of labor is involved, the shop may insist
on the customer paying part (or all) of the normal labor
charge. (This is especially true if the part lasted well beyond the warranty period.)

One shop that I worked in would usually make adjustments on repeat repairs that were past the "official" warranty period. For example, if a part that we had installed
was guaranteed for ninety days and failed after six or sev-
en months, we would replace it and charge the customer

for labor only. Since we had simply exchanged the defective part for a new one with our supplier, we didn't lose any money on the job, and the customer was happy because he got his vehicle repaired without having to pay for a new part.

So, if a repair needs to be done over within a reasonable time after the "official" warranty has expired, insist on some type of adjustment. For repairs that only last one or two months longer than the warranty, you should be able to get a free repair; if it's been three or four months, you may have to pay something (for example, one-half of the normal charge, or labor only).

Don't accept the old excuse, "I'm sorry, but the parts are only guaranteed for ninety days..." If you hear this, tell them that many shops are willing to extend the warranty a few months because they can exchange the parts with their supplier, then ask them why they can't do the same. If they refuse to make any adjustment, tell them that they are going to lose you as a customer, *then find another shop that has a better warranty policy.*

Secret Factory Warranties

When I was working in an independent repair shop, I would occasionally see certain problems on vehicles that had fairly high mileage, so they were definitely out of the official warranty period. However, I knew that these repairs could be done by a dealership at no charge, so I told the customers that they shouldn't pay us to do the work.

Because some of the vehicles had 90-100,000 miles on them (and were six or seven years old), the customers usually thought I was crazy when I said they could go to a dealership to have the repairs done for free. They reluctantly called the dealership and were pleased to hear that they could, in fact, have those repairs done at no charge.

Since I had saved each customer about $300, our shop had just gained several appreciative lifetime customers. So, even though our shop had lost several high-profit repair jobs, sending them to the dealership turned out to be a good public relations move. (It also showed the customers that we were honest.)

"Secret factory warranties" provide free repairs for problems that are common to particular makes or models, even though the official factory warranties have run out. These are known as secret warranties (or "special policy adjustments") because the manufacturers do not publicize them. Vehicle owners are not usually notified that a problem may exist that could be repaired free of charge, even though federal law requires car manufacturers to notify affected consumers and offer free repairs or reimbursement if they've already paid for a covered repair.

Secret warranties normally have a time or mileage limit (usually 1-2 years after the normal warranty has expired), but in some cases free repairs are done with no limitations. For example, Toyota would replace the exhaust manifolds on certain engines free of charge no matter how many miles were on the car. I've seen Toyota dealers perform this warranty repair on cars with 120,000 miles.

Secret warranties don't usually involve safety problems (for example, possible brake failure, or fuel leaks that could cause a fire). Safety problems almost always trigger factory recalls in which all owners of a particular model receive letters informing them of the problem and asking them to bring in the vehicle for free repairs.

How can consumers find out if their vehicle is covered by any secret warranties? The most reliable way is to send a self-addressed, stamped #10 envelope to the Center for Auto Safety, listed in the "Agencies: Who to Call" chapter. Include a note listing the year, make, and model of your vehicle, requesting all the information on factory recalls, vehicle defects, and secret warranties. They will then send you, free of charge, whatever information they have pertaining to your vehicle. The last time I called the Center, they said they had lists for General Motors, Ford, Chrysler, Toyota, Nissan, Hondas, and a few other makes.

Another (less reliable) method is to call the manufacturer's customer service number and ask if they have any "special warranties" that will cover repairs on your vehicle. This number can be found in the vehicle owner's manual and is usually toll-free. If you don't have an owner's manual, ask your local dealership for the number.

Consumers can also ask the people working in a local dealership service department if a repair is covered under a "special warranty," but this is also not very reliable for the same reason as the above method--secret warranties are illegal, so most car companies won't admit that they exist. Also, most dealership personnel are not told about all of the secret warranties, so even if they wanted to let people know (which some of them don't), they're not able to.

If you ask the dealer or manufacturer, and they offer to fix your vehicle for free without a hassle, consider yourself lucky. If they don't, write the Center for Auto Safety to see if the problem is a common one, and whether it's covered by a secret warranty. If it is a common problem, call your manufacturer's customer service number and ask to speak to the district (or zone) manager.

Tell the manager what you received from the Center for Auto Safety, especially if it shows that his company has paid others for the same repair. Ask him if he can get the repairs done under a "special warranty" or "warranty extension." If he says he can't, tell him that you don't think you should have to pay for a major repair so soon after the warranty expired, and that it reflects poorly on his company to have made a vehicle that needs expensive repairs when the mileage is so low.

You can also tell the manager that you know of other car manufacturers (for example, Toyota, Nissan, Honda, etc.) that will repair many items for free even though the official warranty has expired. Tell him that you're going to buy your next car from one of the other companies if you have to pay for the repair.

If you're still not getting anywhere, ask the manager for his name *and* the name and address of the company president; let him know that you're going to write a letter explaining your situation and the fact that your complaints fell on deaf ears. You can also let him know that you're going to pay another repair shop to do the repairs, then you're going to take the manufacturer to small claims court to get your money back.

There's one last threat you can use--tell him you are going to file a complaint with the Federal Trade Commission. (Then do it--don't make empty threats.) The manufacturer will almost always agree to do the repairs for free just to keep the FTC out of the picture.

Remember, the law is on your side--secret warranties are illegal, so the last thing the car companies want to do is have their customers go to the FTC or take them to court. They also don't want to lose customers to their competitors, so make sure you tell them that you're never going to buy one of their cars again if they don't take care of your problem.

Refunds

If you didn't know that a particular repair on your vehicle was covered by a secret warranty and you already paid to have the repairs done, you can usually get reimbursed by the manufacturer for the actual cost of repairs. To do this, you need to speak to the district (or zone) manager, and you'll have to go through the same routine mentioned in the previous paragraphs. Be persistent--this procedure has worked for many people.

Important Note

Just because a repair that your vehicle needs is not on a secret warranty list doesn't necessarily mean that you can't get it done for free. Most of the items on the lists were originally covered only because vehicle owners complained loudly until the repairs were done for free.

So, if a major part fails within several years of the normal warranty expiring, tell them you don't think that part should have failed so soon, and you don't think it's fair for you to have to pay that much money to get it repaired. Let them know that you are not going to give up until they repair it for free (or at least pay for half the cost).

When someone tells you that they can't make any kind of adjustment, ask to speak to their superior. Keep going over their heads until you get results. If you get all the way to the district (or zone) manager and you're told that they're not going to fix it, use the above-mentioned threats about filing a complaint with the FTC and buying your next car from one of their competitors.

It usually helps to have proof that your particular problem is not unusual. The Center for Auto Safety sometimes has statistics on premature failures, and you can also use factory service bulletins as proof that it is a common problem that should be repaired for free. For information on obtaining factory service bulletins, see the listing for the National Highway Traffic Safety Administration in the "Agencies: Who to Call" chapter.

The quickest way for consumers to get all of the service bulletins and recalls on their vehicle is to find a repair shop with an Alldata computerized information system. To have this information printed out usually only costs about $10-15 and can be done in a matter of minutes. To find a shop near you with an Alldata system, call Alldata Corp. at 1-800-829-8727, select "operator."

NISSAN SECRET WARRANTIES

On June 26, 1990, The Detroit News ran a story on the alleged use of "secret warranties" by Nissan Motor Co. Armed with internal Nissan documents leaked by former Nissan employees, the Center for Auto Safety urged the Federal Trade Commission to investigate.

The internal documents were provided by Fred Gramcko, who was Nissan's U.S. director of consumer support from 1982 to 1989, and by Richard Hoffman, Nissan's U.S. director of engineering from 1979 to 1988. The documents show the amounts paid to dealers by Nissan for out-of-warranty repairs on 1982-87 models.

Nissan denied the charges, claiming that the free repair of some out-of-warranty defects was a "goodwill gesture" by the company, not a secret warranty.

According to the Center for Auto Safety, manufacturers are required by federal law to report any repair frequencies that are above normal for a component and offer free repairs or reimbursement for any past expense.

Offering free repairs (or reimbursement) to some but not all vehicle owners is known as a "secret warranty" because there is no public announcement or other notification of the defects and many consumers don't realize they are eligible.

In Nissan's case, the defects were not made public and vehicle owners were not notified. The offer of free repairs did not come until customers complained about the defects.

Nissan "Secret Warranty" List

PULSAR, SENTRA
Fuel pump assembly -- 1983-85.
Vacuum control modulator -- 1984-86.
Rear suspension -- 1984-87.

200SX
Rear spring -- 1986.
Front door finisher -- 1985.

STANZA
Carburetor assembly -- 1983.
Torque converter -- 1984.
Transmission case -- 1983.

STANZA WAGON
Governor assembly -- 1986.
Steering gear rack -- 1986-87.

ZX
Turbocharger -- 1986.
Battery heat shield -- 1985-86.
ATC control assembly -- 1983.
Exhaust gas warning system -- 1985.

TRUCK
Cylinder block -- 1984.
Cylinder head gasket -- 1982.
Transmission case -- 1986.

MAXIMA
Drive plate assembly -- 1986.

Muffler -- 1986.
Alternator -- 1985-86.
Starter -- 1987.
Battery -- 1985.
Head lamp -- 1986.
Fuel level sensor -- 1986.
Compressor assembly -- 1984-85.
Antenna -- 1985-86.
Torque converter -- 1985-87.
Transmission case -- 1986.
Oil pump -- 1985.
Clutch assembly -- 1986.
Sunroof motor -- 1986.
Steering gear -- 1985-87.

Note: This article and list were only included to illustrate how many secret warranties may exist at any time. It is not an exhaustive list (and it is several years old), so be sure to send for a current list if you own a Nissan.

Make sure you send for the lists of defects and secret warranty items for *all* vehicles you've owned for the last two or three years--you may be entitled to a refund for repairs that were done in the past.

TOYOTA SECRET WARRANTIES

On August 26, 1988, The Detroit News ran a story revealing that Toyota Motor Corp. will sometimes offer free out-of-warranty repairs, but only if people ask for them.

A twelve-page Toyota document was leaked anonymously to The News, using company stationery from Toyota's Cincinnati distributor. The document lists 41 components on certain models that Toyota has repaired for free after the warranty has expired.

Bob Daly, Toyota's national service operations manager, confirmed the authenticity of the document, but added that customers usually have to complain about paying for an item that is on the "high frequency of repair" list before the company will offer reimbursement.

Daly also stated that those repairs were done under the company's customer satisfaction policy, and were not examples of "secret warranties."

Upon examination of the Toyota repairs list, the Center for Auto Safety claimed that it "clearly constitutes a secret warranty."

Toyota "Secret Warranty" List

1. Oil filter damage -- 1983 Corollas & Tercels.
2. Camshaft -- Supras & Cressidas.
3. Catalytic convertors -- some light trucks.
4. Cruise control (actuator accelerating) --
     all models, all years.
5. Dashboard pads (cracks, warping) --
     all models, all years.
6. Disc rotors (rust, flaking) -- 1983-86 Tercels.
7. Exhaust manifolds.
8. Exhaust shields.
9. Fuel pumps -- cars only, all years.
10. Fuel tanks (external rust) -- all models, all years.
11. Oil consumption -- all years.
12. Paint peeling (blue only) -- trucks thru 1984.
13. Power train-related -- all 1983-86 models.
14. Rust perforation -- all models thru 1986.
15. Seat back, seat track (bent, warped, deformed) --
     1982 Tercels.
16. Shock absorbers -- some trucks.
17. Speedometer shaft sleeve (oil leak) --
     all models, all years.

18. Thrust washer -- 1983 Celicas, some '83 trucks.
19. Transmission front input shaft bearing (L-52 transmission only) -- four 1981-83 truck models.
20. Universal steering joint -- eight Tercel models.
21. Water pumps -- 1983-84 Camrys.
22. Rear wheel bearings -- 1981-83 Tercels.
23. Rocker arm wear (22-R engine only) -- 1983-84 Celicas & trucks.
24. Truck engines (cylinder wear).
25. Muffler corrosion (loud noise or separation at front pipe) -- Camrys.
26. Horn terminal rust -- some Celicas & Corollas.
27. Paint peeling -- some 1983 Supras, some 1983-84 trucks.
28. Oil sending unit -- Celicas (1983-84 only), vans, trucks, Corollas, Supras, Cressidas.
29. Oil pump gaskets -- Camrys.
30. Front disc brake vibration -- some Camry SV & CV models.
31. Automatic transmission (slippage) -- 1983 Camry SV, 1984 Camry CV, 1985 Corolla CE.
32. Air conditioner compressor lock sensors -- Camrys.
33. Diesel cylinder head gaskets -- Camrys.
34. Lower arm bushing separation -- 1984-86 Camrys.
35. Sulfur odor -- 1984-86 Camrys, Celicas, Tercels.
36. Engine won't start on hill -- 1985-86 Camry SV.
37. Sun roof computer -- 1984-85 Cressidas.
38. Head gaskets -- 1985-86 trucks, 1985 Celicas.
39. Crankshaft and pulley -- vans thru July 1985.
40. Power steering gear-box oil leak -- all Cressidas.
41. Radiator fan motors -- 1983-86 Tercels.

Note: This article and list were only included to illustrate how many secret warranties may exist at any time. It is not an exhaustive list (and it is several years old), so be sure to send for a current list if you own a Toyota.

Make sure you send for the lists of defects and secret warranty items for **all** vehicles you've owned for the last two or three years--you may be entitled to a refund for repairs that were done in the past.

What Auto Mechanics Don't Want You to Know

CHAPTER 14

Finding Mechanics
You Can Trust

Asking friends to recommend a good mechanic is the most common method, but it is not always reliable. I have seen people who were sure they had the best mechanic in town, trusting him for years and recommending him to all of their friends. Their "trusted mechanic" was actually charging them for many unnecessary repairs; he wasn't a well-trained, highly-skilled technician, and was making incorrect guesses as to what was wrong with their vehicle.

Because he was always friendly and charming, though, they believed that he could be trusted; and since he always fixed their vehicle (even though they frequently had to bring it back several times before it was *really* fixed), they thought he was a good mechanic.

How can you tell which repair shop or mechanic can be trusted to give you an honest deal? By looking for characteristics that are common to the best shops and mechanics in the industry. Before you take your vehicle to a shop, use the phone to see how they measure up. The following guidelines are provided to help you--if possible, *all* of the categories below should be considered before a final decision is made.

EDUCATION

The most important consideration should be the education or skill level of the mechanic, based on studying and continuing education classes, not on years of experience. The experience gained from working on cars in the 1960's or 1970's is all but worthless today because 1980-94 vehicles do not even resemble those built 20 or 30 years ago.

An unskilled (i.e. uneducated) mechanic will make a lot more mistakes than an educated one, and he will have to charge his customers for most of his mistakes if he wants to stay in business. For this reason, the consumer has the best chance of not being charged for unnecessary repairs by finding an educated mechanic.

There are several ways to determine a mechanic's level of education. If you are at the repair shop, look on the walls of the office or customer waiting room for certificates and/or licenses that the mechanic has earned. Most community colleges and trade schools issue certificates to mechanics verifying that they have completed a particular course in auto repair. A regular pattern of attendance (at least two or three courses every year) shows that a mechanic is at least trying to keep up with the latest technology. A mechanic who hasn't taken a class in years will not have the knowledge required to properly diagnose and repair late-model vehicles.

Ask the mechanic (or shop owner) what schools or classes he attends, and what trade publications he reads, to keep up with the changing technology. If he says he is able to keep up without going to school or studying, you should look for another mechanic; it's no longer possible for a mechanic to figure out (by himself) everything he needs to know to work on the computer-controlled vehicles built after 1980.

A mechanic's library of repair manuals and other reference books can also be used to indicate his level of education or skill. The average shop repairing the most common domestic and import vehicles needs to buy at least seven or eight manuals every year, so if a shop has been in business for ten years and only has ten or fifteen manuals, I would suspect that the mechanic either hates to read or is not willing to invest the money required to have up-to-date information. Unless you're driving a really old car (twenty-plus years), a shop that doesn't have a lot of books will not be able to properly repair your car.

The manuals used by the most well-trained, highly-skilled technicians are those published by the vehicle manufacturers, and also by Mitchell and Motor. Manuals published by other companies are mostly for "do-it-yourself" mechanics, as they are not usually comprehensive enough for the professional. If a mechanic's library consists mainly of books published by other companies, that can be an indication that he's not very knowledgeable.

Ask the mechanic or shop owner what they do when a vehicle has a problem, and they can't figure it out because everything looks and tests OK. (If he says that never happens, head for the nearest exit--he's lying, because it happens all the time.) Every shop should have a comprehensive set of technical service bulletins (at least 600-700 pages every year), or at least have access to them through a call-in service.

Many late-model vehicles (especially those with computer controls) develop problems that are impossible to diagnose and repair using normal test equipment and procedures. The vehicle manufacturers know these problems exist, so they publish technical service bulletins that explain how to solve them. If a shop doesn't have access to these bulletins, they will be making incorrect guesses when diagnosing many problems, and the vehicle owner will end up paying for unnecessary repairs.

Several fairly new computer systems (made by Alldata Corporation and Mitchell International) have been made especially for repair shops. These systems have most of the repair manuals, labor guides, wiring diagrams, and technical service bulletins on computer disks for easy reference. A shop with one of these systems won't need very many books, since a typical system contains about 200,000 printed pages.

MECHANIC CERTIFICATION

Look for ASE-certified mechanics. "ASE" is the symbol of the National Institute for Automotive Service Excellence, which is a voluntary, national testing program created to help the public identify shops employing knowledgeable mechanics. Certification is not a guarantee that a mechanic is honest or even highly proficient, but it does show that the mechanic is reasonably intelligent and understands the automotive categories he is certified in.

The ASE tests are difficult enough to weed out at least 50% of the mechanics taking them for the first time; many mechanics refuse to take them at all because they don't like taking tests (and are afraid they won't pass). Less than 10% of all mechanics in the country are ASE-certified.

I have taken and passed a number of ASE tests, and can testify that they are not that difficult for a technician who is literate and knows his trade. However, they will definitely eliminate someone who does not have a good understanding of automotive diagnosis and repair.

Don't assume all of the mechanics working in a repair shop are certified in all categories just because the shop displays the ASE symbol. To use the symbol, a shop is only required to have one mechanic who is ASE-certified in one out of eight areas.

When you take your vehicle in for repairs, insist that an ASE-certified technician do all of the work (except for lube and oil changes). If more people would do this, it would encourage shop owners to employ only certified technicians.

The ASE program is excellent, but it does fall short in one area--testing for theory and knowledge concerning engine performance on computer-controlled vehicles. Most of the manufacturers started installing computers in their vehicles between 1979 and 1984, so a mechanic without a thorough understanding of computer systems will not be able to properly diagnose and repair driveability problems on most late-model vehicles.

Until the ASE program begins testing for knowledge of computer system theory, consumers will have to evaluate a mechanic's level of education and skill in this area, using the guidelines mentioned earlier in this chapter.

Almost all new car dealerships employ ASE-certified mechanics, as do many large independent repair shops and chains. Look for the "ASE" symbol in shop advertisements, signs, and patches worn by the mechanics.

QUALITY PARTS

The use of inexpensive parts will almost always result in premature failure, which is not only expensive because the repair did not last as long as it should have, but it can be dangerous if it causes brake failure or stalling in the middle of an intersection or a railroad crossing.

Ask the shop owner what brands of parts they use for brakes, tune ups, electrical (starters, alternators, regulators, etc.), and engine parts--even gaskets. Make sure they are using high-quality, name-brand parts; if you don't recognize the brands he mentions, call an auto parts store that is used by professional mechanics and ask if the brands mentioned are of high quality. (The easiest way to find the name of a good local auto parts store is to call a dealership parts department and ask them for a recommendation.)

Beware of "look-alike" parts, as well as the repair shops that use them. Low-quality, counterfeit parts that resemble name brands are often sold to shops for a fraction of the price of high-quality parts. The boxes that the counterfeit parts come in often use the same designs and colors as those containing name brands, so they appear to be high-quality parts to the uninformed.

Some shop owners buy these "look-alike" parts through the mail from out-of-state telephone solicitors, installing them in their customers' vehicles and charging the same prices that the name brands sell for. By doing this, a shop's profit margin on parts can be 50-70% instead of the normal 25-30% margin.

Insist on the use of high-quality, name-brand parts when your vehicle is repaired. Trying to save money on a brake job by using inexpensive parts can result in injury or even death if the brakes do not work properly. Since labor charges are now the major part of the typical repair bill, the use of inexpensive parts will not save money in the long run because the repair will not last as long as it should have. The cheaper parts always seem to last through the warranty period, leaving the customer to pay the full cost of doing the repair over again.

QUALITY DIAGNOSTIC & REPAIR WORK

If you want honest, high-quality diagnostic and repair work done on your vehicle, expect to pay for it. Because there's a shortage of well-trained, highly-skilled technicians, it's not likely that a shop can find or keep one without paying him a lot. (This is simply the law of supply and demand at work.) In many areas of the country with a high cost of living, a highly-skilled technician can make $15-20 per hour (or more). Add the cost of benefits to his salary and he can end up costing a shop $20-25 per hour.

In addition, a typical shop needs a minimum of $75,000 in equipment to work on late-model vehicles. Equipment payments, rent, utilities, insurance, and other shop expenses can easily add another $10-15 to shop overhead for every working hour. If overhead costs a repair shop $30-40 per hour (before the owner gets paid), they certainly can't afford to work on customers' vehicles without charging for everything they do.

Ask the shop owner if they charge for all diagnostic work, even if they end up doing the repairs. A professional mechanic will not only charge for all diagnostic work, but will refuse to repair a vehicle without first performing diagnostic tests to make sure the repair is necessary.

Beware of shops that offer a free diagnosis--if they know they are not going to be paid for any of the time spent diagnosing your vehicle, they will not want to spend much time checking it out. This will almost always result in unnecessary repairs, because they will be more inclined to "guess" what is wrong instead of testing to pinpoint the problem.

Today's vehicles are so complex that most problems require a minimum of one-half hour for an accurate diagnosis, with many electrical and computer problems requiring several hours. (Note: As outlined in the chapter on brake repairs, the offer of "free inspections" has been used by many shops to bring in new customers who were sold unnecessary repairs.)

Choosing a repair shop because it has the lowest prices is not usually a good idea--comparing prices between shops can be like comparing apples and oranges. A shop may have lower prices because it employs less-skilled mechanics, because it doesn't have up-to-date equipment, or because it uses lower-quality parts than a shop charging higher prices. Also, the repair work of all shops (and even mechanics) is not of the same quality; some just want to finish the job as fast as possible, while others are more concerned about turning out high-quality work.

A mechanic who is in a hurry is far more likely to overlook something that could be a potential problem--if he has to choose between finishing the job quickly and interrupting the job to obtain customer approval for additional parts and/or labor, he will usually choose to finish the job quickly. This practice often results in a repair that does not last as long as it should have, with the customer picking up the tab later on when the repair needs to be done over again (after the warranty expires).

Generally speaking, shops with lower prices tend to put more emphasis on getting the job done quickly, and mechanics who are always in a hurry are more likely to make mistakes that the customer will end up paying for.

REFERENCES

Asking your friends to recommend a mechanic can be a good starting point, but it's not foolproof; there are many incompetent mechanics out there with loyal customers who mistakenly believe their mechanic is giving them a fair deal. To make matters worse, these deceived customers are recommending their mechanic to all of their friends. If you do ask your friends for a recommendation, make sure the other categories listed in this chapter are checked also.

If the mechanics that you and your friends have been

using fail any of these categories, especially the first three, resist the temptation to stay with the mechanics you know, even if they don't measure up. Remember, an educated mechanic will make fewer mistakes that you'll end up paying for.

Checking references on a repair shop that neither you nor any of your friends have used before is fairly simple. Several methods can be used, depending on how fast you need the information. (Keep in mind that any shop that has been in business for a while is bound to have some complaints against it, but there should not be a huge number of them.) The quickest way to find out how many complaints have been made against a shop (and more important, how those complaints were resolved) is to call the local Better Business Bureau.

The state Department of Consumer Affairs can also provide information on repair shops, but they usually require that requests be made in writing. Look in the phone book under "state government" listings for the agency nearest you. (In California, call the state Bureau of Automotive Repair.) The *Consumers Resource Handbook*, a federal government publication, lists all consumer agency contacts for not only automotive repair, but all other categories as well; it also lists a number of automotive publications as well. This free booklet can be obtained by calling (719) 948-4000 or writing to:

Consumer Information Center
Pueblo, CO 81009

An excellent method of getting referrals for auto repair is to call the local AAA office, which will give out (over the phone) the names of several shops in your area that are AAA Approved Auto Repair facilities.

Before a shop can qualify as a AAA Approved facility, it must meet AAA's standards for qualified personnel, customer service, necessary tools and equipment, good reputation, shop appearance, and insurance. AAA checks references from previous customers (taken at random from the shop's files), requiring a favorable response from at least 85% of those questioned.

To be in the AAA program, a shop must be approved in the following areas: engine tune-up, brakes, electrical systems, minor engine repair, and either heating/air conditioning or tires/steering/suspension. Optional areas include: major engine repairs, automatic transmission, manual transmission, and diagnostic lane.

A major advantage in using a AAA Approved shop is their binding arbitration policy (for members only), which can save a customer the time and expense of going to court to resolve a complaint. One of the conditions of AAA approval is that the shops must accept AAA's decision regarding complaints. Customers with a complaint against an approved shop are encouraged to let AAA resolve the problem.

After interviewing the customer and the mechanic, reviewing the estimate and repair order, and road testing the vehicle to determine how well the job was done, a AAA representative (with a background in the auto repair business) will decide how the problem should be resolved. He may tell the shop to refund part or all of the amount charged for the repair, or he may tell the customer that a refund is not justified. AAA's decision is binding on the repair facility, but not on the customer, who is free to take the shop to court if he is not satisfied with the decision.

If AAA decides against a shop and they refuse to refund the customer's money, AAA will pay the customer the amount decided. Since all approved shops agreed to honor AAA's decision as a condition of approval, a shop's refusal to refund a customer's money can result in AAA dropping that shop from its list of approved repair facilities.

Because of this policy, if you are considering using a shop that was AAA-approved at one time but is not any longer, it would be a good idea to find out why they dropped out of the program. Some shop owners have told customers that they voluntarily dropped out because they were "tired of the paperwork" or "it wasn't worth the trouble," when the truth was that AAA dropped them from the program because they had too many complaints and/or refused to refund a customer's money when AAA rendered a decision against the shop.

Since the AAA program basically checks most of the categories listed in this chapter, it can be used as a shortcut instead of doing the checking yourself. However, AAA's examination of a shop may not be as thorough and critical as if you had done it yourself, especially in the areas of mechanics' education and certification.

AAA allows an "equivalent" to ASE certification, and will approve a shop without certification if the shop agrees to obtain it within two testing periods. AAA does require a formal training system for keeping employees up-to-date, but does not specify what type of classes mechanics must attend or how often. A major drawback to using this shortcut, besides the education and certification issues, is that many reputable repair shops are not in the AAA program and may be overlooked.

It should be emphasized that a AAA Approved Repair facility is not guaranteed to be perfect or even the best shop in town, but has simply met the minimum standards established by AAA. If you decide to use the AAA program to locate a repair shop, I recommend that you get the names of several shops in your area from AAA and choose one that meets the education and certification standards outlined in this chapter. (Unfortunately, this program is only in about 30 states at this time.)

Another shortcut to finding good repair shops is to ask the auto parts stores that cater to the professionals (like Napa Auto Parts), rather than the "do-it-yourselfers."

SHOP EQUIPMENT

A typical repair shop needs to have at least $75,000 in equipment and tools for proper diagnosis and repair of late-model vehicles in the areas of tune up, electrical, air conditioning, brakes, and minor engine repair.

Without the proper equipment, a mechanic is forced to guess what the cause of the problem is instead of testing for it, which almost always results in the customer paying for unnecessary repairs. Also, if a shop does not have easy access to the equipment required to do a thorough repair job, they will be more inclined to take shortcuts that result in a repair not lasting as long as it should have.

For example, on some late-model computer-controlled vehicles, a malfunctioning alternator can cause erratic engine operation by affecting the computer. This can happen without causing the alternator light to come on or the battery to go dead, so the alternator would not normally be suspect. A mechanic can properly diagnose this problem in about 20 minutes using one of the new computerized engine analyzers (that sell for about $30,000).

Without that analyzer, several hours might be wasted, and the computer might be replaced unnecessarily, before the problem is properly diagnosed. This is how a repair that should only cost $150-200 ends up being $300-400.

If a shop does not have a brake lathe to resurface drums and rotors, they'll have to send them out to a machine shop. This situation often results in the mechanic deciding not to resurface the drums and/or rotors because he doesn't want to wait for them. (It's not unusual for a shop to wait all day for the drums or rotors to come back from the machine shop, resulting in a rack being tied up that is needed for other vehicles.) Also, if the shop is doing a brake job over again (for free) to resolve a complaint, they will not want to pay to have the parts resurfaced.

Failure to resurface the drums and/or rotors when the brakes are relined often results in poor brake performance--for example, a pulsating brake pedal or front end shimmy when braking, noisy brakes, or a brake reline that does not last as long as it should have.

Ask the shop owner or mechanic to give you a tour of the shop and show you their equipment. A shop that does tune-up and diagnostic work should have one of the new computerized engine analyzers mentioned above, along with a digital volt/ohmmeter and an exhaust analyzer. If they do electrical work, they should have a volt/ohm/amp tester; a battery charger and load tester; and an alternator/ regulator/starter circuit tester.

For brake work, a shop should have a brake drum and disc lathe, dial indicators, and micrometers. For air conditioning work, a gauge set, leak detector, recharging station, and vacuum pump are needed. A shop that does tires, steering, and suspension work should have an alignment rack, a dynamic (spin-type) wheel balancer, and a tire changer.

CLEAN ORGANIZED SHOP

The repair shop should be reasonably clean and orderly for two reasons. First, mechanics working in a grimy shop tend to leave grease stains inside customers' vehicles, which most people don't appreciate. Second, many repairs require that the vehicle (or part of the vehicle) be disassembled for long periods of time, and if the shop is disorganized, the mechanic may not be able to find some of the parts when he is ready to reassemble the vehicle.

When this happens, the customer is usually told that the repair is going to cost "a little more than we originally thought because another part needs to be replaced." (I have also seen mechanics assemble a vehicle *without* the missing part, hoping that no one would notice. Of course, the vehicle was brought back later to have the job done over because it didn't function properly.)

CUSTOMER SERVICE

A safe, clean, and comfortable customer waiting area should be provided. All customer service personnel should be knowledgeable and courteous, willing to explain the necessary tests and repairs in language the average person can understand.

A signed, written estimate should be required before any work is begun. Customer approval must be obtained for any additional repairs that will exceed the original estimate. All parts installed should be identified by part number and a notation indicating whether they are new, rebuilt, or used.

When requested, all replaced parts should be returned to the customer, preferably in the boxes that the new parts came in so the brand names can be checked for quality. The only legitimate excuse for not returning the old parts is to avoid a core charge. If this is the case, the old parts can still be returned if the customer pays the core charge. After examining the old parts to make sure replacement was necessary, the customer can return the parts for a refund or credit.

All repairs should be guaranteed in writing for at least 90 days or 4,000 miles; there should be no parts or labor charges for repairs done under warranty.

CHAPTER 15

Agencies: Who to Call

AUTO REPAIR COMPLAINTS

CALIFORNIA--
Bureau of Automotive Repair
10240 Systems Parkway
Sacramento, CA 95827
Calif. only (800) 952-5210
All others (916) 445-1254

MICHIGAN--
Bureau of Automotive Regulation
208 N. Capitol Ave.
Lansing, MI 48918
Mich. only (800) 292-4204
All others (313) 357-5108

ALL OTHER STATES--
Contact your state Consumer Protection Agency,
or the state Attorney General's office

For complaints against auto repair shops, call or write the appropriate agency for your state. Complaint forms can usually be requested by phone. Action can be taken for obvious violations of a state's laws or regulations. If numerous complaints are filed against one shop, an investigation may be started.

Complaints can also be made to your local Better Business Bureau and city/county District Attorney's consumer protection division.

FACTORY RECALLS, SAFETY DEFECTS, & SERVICE BULLETINS--

National Highway Traffic Safety Administration
400 7th Street SW, Room 5110
Washington, DC 20590
(800) 424-9393

The NHTSA collects information on all automotive recalls (including child safety seats), safety defects and complaints, crash tests, standards for all automotive parts, and factory service bulletins covering all vehicles sold in the United States. Will research service bulletins to locate those explaining a manufacturer's solution to a difficult repair problem. Has certified data and films on crash tests.

On GM, FORD, and VW vehicles, factory service bulletin information can also be obtained by calling the following manufacturers' toll-free customer service numbers:
GM (800) 551-4123; FORD (800) 241-3673;
VW (800) 544-8021.

If you need to get recall or service bulletin information immediately, any repair shop with an Alldata computerized information system can print them out for you (typical charge: $10-15). To locate a shop near you, call Alldata Corp. at (800) 829-8727, select "operator."

SECRET WARRANTIES, VEHICLE DEFECTS, SAFETY RECALLS, & LEMON LAWS--

Center for Auto Safety
2001 S Street NW, Suite 410
Washington, DC 20009
(202) 328-7700

The Center for Auto Safety is a non-profit clearing house for information on secret warranties, vehicle defects, recalls, lemon laws, and attorney referral to lemon law specialists. To receive information, send a self-addressed, stamped envelope to the Center with a note listing the year, make, and model of your vehicle. Don't forget to specify what kind of information you need. (Normal response time is 3-4 weeks.)

MEDIATION & ARBITRATION--

Autocap
National Automobile Dealers Association
8400 Westpark Drive
McLean, VA 22102
(703) 821-7144

Third party mediation for anything related to vehicle manufacturers or dealers. Arbitration is also available for unresolved problems.

The Better Business Bureau and AAA also have arbitration programs for some manufacturers, dealers, and repair shops. Contact your local BBB or AAA office for details.

EMISSION WARRANTIES--

Environmental Protection Agency
401 M Street SW
Washington, DC 20460
(202) 233-9040

The EPA has complete information on all vehicle emission warranties, gas mileage data for all vehicles, and import/export emission information.

CHAPTER 16

Vehicle Maintenance "Secrets"

Many people have heard stories of how some guy put 200,000 miles (or more) on his car without any major repairs, stories that are often dismissed as "dumb luck" or just plain fabrications. Granted, some of the stories may have been exaggerated, but it's very possible to put at least 150,000 miles on a car without major engine or transmission repairs. I've done this several times, and so have many of the customers whose cars I've worked on. In this chapter, you will learn the "secrets" to getting the most out of your vehicle without having to pay for major repairs.

The first "secret" is:

READ THE OWNER'S MANUAL!!

This tip should not be a "secret" to anyone, but many people don't read and follow the maintenance schedule in their owner's manual, then they complain when they have to pay for major repairs because their car wasn't properly maintained.

For those of you who claim you "can't remember" to perform scheduled maintenance on your vehicle, try writing yourself brief notes such as, "change oil," "tune-up," etc., on your calendar where you estimate the work should be done based on time or mileage. Also, go to a stationery store and buy an auto record book (cost: about $1.50) to record the date and mileage of all maintenance work and repairs.

If you bought a used vehicle and the owner's manual is missing, ask a local dealership that sells that type of vehicle where you might find one; if that doesn't work, go to a library, bookstore, or major magazine distributor to look at the classified ads in several auto magazines. There are many car clubs and collectors of old manuals who would probably have the one you are looking for.

The second "secret" is: *Never* drive your vehicle when it's really low on oil or water, or when the engine temperature or oil pressure gauges read in the danger zone (indicating an overheating or low oil pressure condition). As a mechanic, I have seen hundreds of blown-up engines, and almost all of them were out of water or oil (or both).

Even if your engine doesn't blow up immediately after it's driven without oil or water, it will have already suffered serious damage, drastically reducing its useful lifespan. This is why some people end up paying for an engine overhaul at 75,000 miles or less while others (who never ran out of oil or water) are still driving around with the original engine at 150,000 miles.

If you are driving your vehicle and the temperature gauge suddenly drops to the "cold" side, pull over as quickly as possible and check the coolant level in the radiator--all of the coolant may have just leaked out.

On some vehicles, it's possible to overheat the engine without it registering on the temperature gauge if all of the coolant suddenly leaks out. This can happen if the temperature sending unit needs to be immersed in liquid to measure the coolant temperature (which is a rather poor design, I might add).

The third "secret" is that there are no short-cuts for properly maintaining a vehicle, but the end results are definitely worth the effort. For example, I have seen many automatic transmissions that lasted at least 130,000 miles without any major repairs because the fluid was changed every 25-30,000 miles. On the other hand, as a mechanic, I have replaced many transmissions in customers' vehicles at only 70-80,000 miles because they had never been serviced. Regular maintenance can double the useful life of a $1500 transmission.

As a general rule, all of the items listed in the maintenance schedule of the owner's manual should be serviced *at least* as often as the manufacturer recommends. I would change the oil and filter more frequently, and also some of the other items if the vehicle is operated under severe conditions. (See the following sections for more details.)

It's always easier (and less expensive) to have a vehicle worked on at your convenience than it is to wait until it breaks down, which can result in a towing bill and serious engine or transmission damage. Since many parts on a vehicle will not last forever, replacing them near the end of their expected lifespan can prevent the inconvenience and expense of a breakdown.

For example, if you live in an area that has cold winters, and your four-year battery is almost four years old in the fall, replacing it before winter arrives would be a wise thing to do since the odds are that the battery would not make it through the winter.

The following sections list maintenance services that should be performed more frequently than some manufacturers recommend. When applicable, "severe operating conditions" include: towing a trailer; driving on rough, dusty, or muddy roads; driving in severe hot or cold weather; frequent stop-and-go driving; repeated short distance driving.

Checking Under the Hood

The oil and coolant levels should be checked at every other fill-up (or two weeks). Add fluids if necessary; check for leaks if any fluid levels are low and repair as needed. *Keep an eye on the oil level*--don't let it drop below the "add" line, or serious engine damage may result. If the engine leaks or burns oil, check it frequently--every day, if necessary. (Yes, I know this is inconvenient, but not as much as an engine that blew up because it ran out of oil.)

If your vehicle has an automatic transmission, check its fluid level once a month. Watch for fluid discoloration or a burnt odor, as these are usually signs of transmission overheating or internal problems. Service if necessary.

Other items that should be checked once a month include the drive belts and coolant hoses, the brake fluid level, and (if equipped) the power steering and clutch cylinder fluid levels.

Check the air filter every 2 to 3 months and replace if necessary. Depending on driving conditions, air filters usually last 10-15,000 miles before they need to be replaced.

Lube, Oil, & Filter Change

Most of the vehicle manufacturers recommend a lube, oil, and filter change at 7,500 miles, a figure that is higher than the one recommended several years ago. The manufacturers claim that the higher figure is justified due to improvements in the oil, but today's vehicles also run much hotter than the older ones did, which causes the oil to break down faster.

I am slightly skeptical of the higher figure because the manufacturers have no incentive to help their customers get 150,000 miles or more out of their vehicles instead of only 100,000. After all, they are in the business of selling as many new vehicles as possible and they would lose a lot of money if everyone kept their vehicles 50% longer, instead of buying new ones.

A lube, oil, and filter change should be done *at least* every 4,000 to 5,000 miles (4 to 5 months) under normal conditions, and every 3,000 miles (3 months) under severe conditions. Make sure the filter is changed along with the oil, otherwise a quart of dirty oil is left in the engine.

Use only high-quality, name-brand filters and oil. It's not worth risking an engine to save a few dollars buying inexpensive parts. (Many of the cheaper filters do not filter the oil as well as the name-brand ones.) Follow the manufacturer's recommendations for oil type and grade.

Cooling System Service

The cooling system is often neglected by most drivers until the vehicle overheats; unfortunately, by the time someone notices that something is wrong, the engine may already be seriously damaged. As a mechanic, I have seen hundreds of engines that had to be replaced because they were driven while they were overheated. To prevent this from happening to you, make sure that the cooling system is in good condition and that it always has the proper coolant level.

Most radiator hoses, heater hoses, and drive belts have an average lifespan of about three years, so when they are around three years old, it's not a bad idea to replace all of them at the same time. (This may be necessary every two years under extreme conditions, such as prolonged hot weather or towing a trailer.) This will prevent repeated changing of the hoses or belts, one at a time, as they fail. After replacing the drive belts, put the old ones in the trunk just in case you need one someday when you are out on the highway.

The recommended interval for flushing the radiator and replacing the coolant is every 2 to 3 years (depending on driving conditions), so make sure this is done at the same time the radiator and heater hoses are replaced to save money.

If you see any drops or puddles of coolant on the ground where your vehicle is parked, open the hood and check the coolant level in the recovery bottle and radiator. *Never remove the radiator cap on a hot engine,* or you may end up in the burn ward at the local hospital.

Before removing the radiator cap, squeeze the upper radiator hose to make sure the engine has cooled and the system is not under pressure. If the hose feels hot and "inflated," don't remove the cap yet--the system is still under pressure. Wait until the hose feels cool and not "inflated" anymore, then slowly turn the radiator cap (counterclockwise), pausing at the safety notch to release any residual pressure before removing the cap completely.

Almost all manufacturers recommend checking the coolant level in the plastic coolant recovery bottle instead of taking the radiator cap off and checking the level in the radiator. (They usually say not to remove the radiator cap at all, but to check and add all coolant at the recovery bottle.)

There are two reasons for this recommendation. The first is that a properly-operating cooling system (with no leaks and a good radiator cap) will have a full radiator when the level in the coolant recovery bottle is correct. The second reason is safety--a person can be severely burned removing a radiator cap on a hot engine if they don't know what they are doing.

However, failure to check the coolant level in the radiator can result in overheating and serious engine damage if the cooling system develops a leak or the radiator cap fails to work properly. When this happens, there will not be any suction to draw the coolant out of the recovery bottle and into the radiator, resulting in an empty radiator even though the recovery bottle is full. *Don't assume that the radiator level is all right just because the coolant recovery bottle is full.*

Checking the levels in the radiator and the recovery bottle is also a good way to tell whether the cooling system is sealed properly--if the radiator level has dropped, but the level in the recovery bottle has not, the system should be tested for leaks or a defective radiator cap.

Tires

Tire pressures should be checked regularly, making sure they are fully inflated when cold. Underinflation by as little as 2-3 lbs. will not only reduce the life of the tire, but will also increase fuel consumption and affect vehicle handling.

Check your owner's manual or call a tire dealer for the correct tire pressure for your vehicle. (The pressure that is listed on the side of the tire is the *maximum* tire pressure, beyond which the tire may blow out if driven at high speeds for an extended period of time. This is not necessarily the ideal pressure for that tire on your vehicle.)

If most of your driving is done at freeway speeds, add 2 lbs. to the recommended tire pressure, but *do not* exceed the maximum pressure listed on the side of the tire.

To extend the life of your tires, have them rotated (from front to rear only) every 5-6,000 miles. Have this done at the same time as a lube, oil, and filter change to save money. (If your vehicle is already up on a hoist for an oil change, the charge for a tire rotation should only be a fraction of the normal price.)

While they are rotating the tires, have them check the brakes. (It only takes a minute to check the brakes when the wheels are already off, so there shouldn't be an extra charge for this.) Ask the mechanic how the tires look and whether they indicate the need for any adjustments or repairs (for example, shock absorbers or alignment).

Whenever new tires are installed on the front of a vehicle, the front end should be checked for worn parts, and the alignment should be checked and adjusted if necessary. If this is not done, uneven tire wear may result, shortening the useful life of the tires.

Annual (Safety) Inspection

To prevent unnecessary breakdowns, and to catch problems before they become major ones, have your mechanic inspect your vehicle once a year. (You can save money by having this done at the same time as an oil change, tire rotation, and brake inspection, since many items would be checked anyway as a part of those services.)

The purpose of the inspection is to visually check all mechanical and electrical systems on a vehicle for any signs of potential problems such as cracked brake hoses, fluid leaks, rust holes in the exhaust system, leaking or worn shock absorbers, unusual tire wear, worn front end parts, corrosion build-up on battery terminals, frayed electrical wires, burnt transmission fluid, etc.

A visual inspection of this type should only take about 30 minutes, so the cost should be about $30 (or less). If a serious problem is discovered, more time may be required for disassembly and diagnosis, but you can tell the mechanic that you only want him to spend 30 minutes on the inspection unless he calls you for approval.

Engine Tune-up

Due to improvements in automotive and gasoline technology, today's vehicles require fewer engine tune-ups than those built before the 1980's. Also, fewer parts need to be replaced when a tune-up is done--there are no more points and condensers to replace due to widespread use of electronic ignition, and improvements in distributor cap design have generally eliminated the need to replace them with every tune-up. (Some models don't even have a distributor, so there's no rotor or cap to replace.)

Most late-model vehicles can usually go at least 25-30,000 miles between minor tune-ups. Since no two vehicles or drivers are alike, keep track of the mileage between tune-ups and ask the mechanic if you should bring the vehicle in sooner or later for the next one.

A minor tune-up should include replacement of the spark plugs, fuel filter, rotor, and (cleaning or replacing) the PCV valve. The distributor cap, spark plug wires, air filter, and breather element should be checked and replaced if necessary. Insist on the use of high-quality, name-brand parts. After all necessary parts have been replaced, the engine should be tested on an analyzer to make sure no other problems exist and to adjust the timing, idle speed, and air/fuel ratio (if possible).

In spite of what the commercials say, using a particular brand of gasoline will not always keep all fuel injectors perfectly clean. If your fuel-injected vehicle has quite a few miles on it, and it isn't starting or running as well as it did before, it may need to have the injectors professionally cleaned to restore peak performance. Ask your mechanic if he thinks your vehicle would benefit from this service. (If your vehicle has throttle body injection, he can easily check the injector spray pattern with a timing light to determine whether the injector needs to be serviced.)

One last tip: *A tune-up will not cure all driveability problems.* If your engine is running rough, don't take it to your mechanic and tell him that it needs a tune-up; tell him it's running rough and you want him to check it out. It may only need a spark plug wire that costs about $7, or it may need major engine work that a tune-up wouldn't fix. In either case, tuning the engine would have been a waste of time and money.

Valve Adjustment

Most four cylinder (and some six cylinder) engines have adjustable valves that should be inspected periodically and adjusted if necessary. Failure to have this done can result in burnt valves, which means that the engine will need a valve job costing $500-800. Recommended time intervals for this service vary from one car manufacturer to the next (usually 15-30,000 miles) so be sure to check the owner's manual for the correct interval.

Automatic Transmission Service

Automatic transmissions should be serviced at least every 25-30,000 miles, 10-15,000 miles if the vehicle is used to pull a trailer. The service should include draining and refilling the transmission (and torque converter, if possible) with new fluid, a new filter, band adjustment (if applicable), and a visual inspection for leaks or other potential problems.

Watch for transmission fluid leaks; repair them before they become a major problem. If the fluid level gets too low, the transmission may slip in and out of gear, or it may not go into gear at all. Transmission damage may result if the vehicle is operated when the fluid is low.

Manual Transmission/Transaxle Service

Change the fluid in the manual transmission or transaxle at 25-30,000-mile intervals, more often if recommended by the manufacturer or the vehicle is used to pull a trailer.

Check the fluid level and inspect for leaks at every oil change. Repair any leaks as soon as they are discovered; operating the vehicle without fluid will quickly destroy the transmission or transaxle.

The clutch adjustment should be checked every 7,500 miles/6 months under normal conditions, or 3,000 miles/3 months if the vehicle is operated under severe conditions. Adjust if necessary to maintain proper free-play (usually at least 3/8-1/2"). Failure to maintain proper free-play will cause premature clutch failure.

Differential Service

Change the fluid in the differential at 50,000-mile intervals, more often if recommended by the manufacturer or the vehicle is used to pull a trailer.

On some vehicles, it may not be possible to drain the differential without major disassembly. If this is the case, use a siphoning device to remove as much fluid as possible through the fill hole, then refill the differential with new fluid.

Check the fluid level and inspect for leaks at every oil change. Repair any leaks as soon as they are discovered; operating the vehicle without fluid will quickly destroy the differential.

Air Conditioning

Routine servicing of the air conditioning system is not usually necessary. If a large amount of bugs and/or leaves becomes stuck in the condenser (in front of the radiator), they should be blown out with compressed air.

Be sure to run the air conditioner for several minutes at least once a week, especially during the winter when it normally wouldn't be used for months. It needs to be run periodically to keep the seals from drying out and to lubricate other internal parts. Failure to do this can result in major repair bills to restore the air conditioning system.

Repair any leaks as soon as they are discovered, because the oil in the system leaks out along with the refrigerant. If too much oil leaks out, and the system is run, the compressor will be damaged.

I don't recommend using do-it-yourself recharging kits--if proper procedures are not followed when servicing an air conditioner, serious injury can result. Also, poor cooling and/or component damage can result from air that enters the system (because it wasn't purged from the hose), or from an overcharge of refrigerant.

Timing Belts

For vehicles equipped with rubber timing belts (mostly 4 cylinder engines), most manufacturers recommend replacement at 50-60,000 miles. If there is no recommendation, replace it anyway. This item is extremely important; failure to replace the timing belt when recommended can result in major towing and repair bills if the belt breaks when the engine is running.

MAINTENANCE SUMMARY

Although most vehicle owners know that scheduled maintenance must be done to keep the warranty in force, few people realize that it's not necessary to have it done at a dealership. Some dealerships lead people to believe that it's required so they won't go to another shop, but it's against the law to require that any scheduled maintenance (to keep a warranty in force) be done at the shop issuing the warranty if the consumer has to pay for the maintenance. (This applies to all automotive warranties, not just those issued by the car manufacturers.) A dealership or independent shop issuing a warranty can require that all warranty work be done at their shop, though, if it is being done at no charge.

Consumers can usually save a significant amount of money by having their scheduled maintenance done at qualified independent repair shops instead of dealerships. To maintain the warranty, take your owner's manual to the shop so they will know what services are required, and make sure they write on the repair order what was done (for example, "15,000 mile service," "30,000 mile service," etc.) Copies of all repair orders showing that the maintenance was done is all that is required to maintain an automotive warranty.

Maintaining the proper fluid levels in your vehicle, in addition to regular maintenance and periodic inspections, can prevent the need for most major repairs. Few engines would ever need replacing if the oil and coolant levels were checked every day, but most people wouldn't be willing to do this. So, the next best thing is to develop a new habit that requires practically no effort. In addition to checking the oil and coolant levels at every fill-up (or every 2 weeks), try to put into practice the following trick.

Whenever possible, park your vehicle in the same spot every day. Make it a habit to check the pavement for any signs of a leak under your vehicle. (You may have to clean the area first in order to notice any new leaks.) This way, you probably won't get caught driving around without any oil or coolant in the engine because it started leaking a week ago and you didn't notice.

If you see any drops or puddles of fluid on the ground where your vehicle is parked, open the hood and check the levels using the dipstick or removing the cap. *Don't forget--never remove the radiator cap on a hot engine;* wait for the engine to cool first.

CHAPTER 17

What Car Salesmen Don't Want You to Know

Most new car buyers pay hundreds (sometimes thousands) of dollars more than they have to because they don't know what the dealer paid for their car and they're not prepared to deal with a professional salesman. This chapter was added to give consumers the information they need to get the lowest possible price on the vehicle of their choice, and for those who hate dealing with salesmen, but don't want to pay too much for a new car, a brief explanation is given on how to have a professional car buyer do the negotiating for you. A section on buying used cars can be found at the end of this chapter.

The Truth About "Dealer Cost"

The "factory invoice" is not always the true dealer's cost on a particular vehicle. While it is true that a dealer buys his cars based on the factory invoice price, he'll usually qualify for one or two checks from the manufacturer after the car is sold. These checks represent the "dealer holdback" and "factory-to-dealer cash incentives."

Dealer holdback is a specific percentage or dollar amount that the manufacturer holds back from the dealer until a car is sold. The holdback allows a dealer to make an additional profit (of $300-$600 or more) that's not reflected in his "invoice cost." This explains why some dealers are willing to show buyers the factory invoice, especially if the dealer is also eligible for a factory-to-dealer cash incentive. Holdbacks are not based on volume, so the actual amount is the same at all dealers selling the same model.

All of the domestic manufacturers (General Motors, Ford, & Chrysler) have dealer holdbacks based on 3% of the Manufacturers Suggested Retail Price (also called "MSRP" or "sticker price"). This gives a dealer an additional profit of $600 on a car with an MSRP of $20,000.

Some of the import manufacturers have begun offering holdback money to their dealers to help them remain competitive and profitable. Because this is a fairly recent development, and something the car companies do not want to become public knowledge, there may be holdbacks that are unknown outside the company. When in doubt, make offers assuming a holdback of at least 2% (of MSRP) exists on the car you want, and offer to pay factory invoice (or $300-400 over)--less if the dealer is getting a dealer incentive.

BMW, Jaguar, Mazda, and Volkswagen all have dealer holdbacks of 2% based on MSRP. Isuzu, Nissan, Saab, and Subaru have holdbacks of 3% based on MSRP. The Mitsubishi holdback is 2% of the dealer (factory) invoice. Volvo holdbacks are fixed dollar amounts: $600 on the 240 series, $700 on the 850 series, and $900 on the 940/960 series.

Factory-to-dealer cash incentives also allow dealers to make additional profits that would not be reflected in the spread between the factory invoice and the sales price. The dealer is not required to share this with a buyer, so don't expect him to tell you about it. (He may not even tell his salespeople.)

The dollar amounts of dealer incentives vary and are changed periodically, so consumers need to call a service that keeps track of factory invoices, rebates, and dealer incentives (listed under "Information Sources" in this chapter). Typical incentives range from $500 to $2,000 per car, which is additional profit for the dealer, so this information is crucial if you want to get the best deal.

How Dealers Make Money

New car dealers have many ways to make money on the sale of a new car: the "spread" between the factory invoice and your purchase price, the dealer holdback, factory-to-dealer cash incentives, "back-end sales," and your trade-in (if any).

A dealer often makes most of his profit on the "back end," which means the items or services they talk you into paying for *after* you've agreed on the price of the car. These sales are made by the finance and insurance (F&I) man, who's often one of the highest paid salesmen in a dealership. If you're not prepared for his sales pitch, he can quickly add several thousand dollars to the price of your new car.

Last, but not least, a dealer will always try to make money on your trade-in, by giving you a price that's actually below true wholesale. (This is especially true if you've negotiated a low-profit price on the new car.) Many dealers even have two different books to show what cars are worth--one with lower values to use when they're buying a car, and one with higher values to use when they're selling one.

Make sure you know what your car is worth before you go shopping; better yet, sell it yourself. You should be able to get a lot more money that way, since a dealer usually buys below true wholesale, so he can resell it at or above retail. Beware of dealers offering high prices on trade-ins; it usually means you're paying too much for the new car.

"Back-end Sales"--The Aftersell

As mentioned previously, back-end sales are made by the F&I man after the purchase price has been agreed upon. Typical high-profit back-end items include: dealer financing, rustproofing/undercoating, paint sealer, fabric protection, pinstriping, extended warranties, and credit life or credit disability insurance.

Unless your credit is so bad that you can't get a car loan anywhere else, or the factory is offering below-market financing, you will end up paying a lot more if you use a dealer to finance your car. On a 48 month $12,000 loan, you'll pay $274 more in interest for each additional percentage point (and most dealers will usually try to charge you 2% over the going rate, which will cost you $548 more in interest over the life of the loan). Don't fall for that old line, "It will only cost a few more cents per month; is that worth all the time and effort to arrange your own financing?" *Yes, it is.*

Have your car loan pre-approved through your credit union or bank before you start negotiating, and you'll save yourself a lot of money. Credit unions usually offer the lowest rates, but shop around before you make a decision. If nothing else, at least you'll know whether the dealer's rate is a good deal or a bad one.

Never buy credit life or credit disability insurance from a car dealer; they're grossly overpriced. Even if you do want it (and you probably don't need it), you can definitely buy it from your insurance agent for a lot less. Don't be pressured into buying these--it's against the law for a lender to require you to buy them before making a loan.

Rustproofing/undercoating, paint sealer, fabric protection, and pinstriping are favorite high-profit back-end items for the F&I man. They cost the dealer very little (usually 10-20% of what they'll charge you for them), and in many cases, they're unnecessary or totally worthless. Don't be tricked into paying for any of these.

Why pay $200-400 to rustproof a car that has a 7 year/100,000 mile corrosion warranty, especially when studies have shown that newer cars are far less susceptible to rust than older ones? A 1985 study of 5- and 6-year-old cars in Michigan found 20% with rust perforation. In 1989, less than 3% were found with perforations, and few of the cars inspected ever had rustproofing/undercoating done.

If you really want extra fabric protection, buy several cans of Scotchguard® at the drug store (for about $10) and do it yourself--don't pay $100 or more for something that might not even be done.

Extended Warranties

Auto repair costs keep going up every year, especially for the high-tech engines, transmissions, and computer systems found on late-model cars. Transmission overhauls on many cars can cost $1500 or more, and it's not unusual for a computer repair to cost anywhere from $400 to $800. Because of this, many people are buying extended warranties to cover major repair costs after the original warranty expires (usually 3 years/36,000 miles).

Unfortunately, thousands of people have bought warranties that turned out to be worthless because the warranty company went out of business, or it simply refused to pay for many repairs that should have been covered. To prevent this from happening to you, don't buy an extended warranty unless it's backed by the car manufacturer.

Here's a well-kept secret regarding extended warranties--their prices are negotiable because they have huge profit margins! If you want one, offer to pay 50% of the "list price," and if they say they can't do that (which isn't true), tell them you know you have one year to buy an extended warranty on a new car and you'll just buy one later from someone else. A smart salesman knows that a small profit is better than no profit at all.

If you really want the extended warranty, but they turned down your 50% offer and you need to include it in the financing to pay for it, you could tell them that you're not going to buy the car unless they give you a good deal on the warranty. A smart salesman will accept a lower profit (or sometimes no profit) on one small item if that's what it takes to save a big sale. Or you could wait until the negotiating is almost over and tell them you'll buy the warranty for 60% of the list price.

Tricks Salesmen Use

If a car salesman identifies you as a "payment buyer" or a "trade-in buyer," you are in big trouble. Once you mention that you are concerned about your "monthly payment" or "trade-in," you are marked as a sucker who can be grossly overcharged in many parts of the purchase and not even notice as long as his monthly payment or trade-in is acceptable.

How this works is fairly simple--John Q. Public mentions that he wants $2,000 for his trade-in (that even he knows is only worth $600 retail), and the salesman will figure out a way to make $3,000 or $4,000 profit from John's new car purchase even though he "gave" him $2,000 for his trade-in. John will end up paying the sticker price on the new car, his interest rate will be higher, there will be a number of overpriced or worthless ("back-end") options added to the car, he'll pay $180 for "processing," $400 for "dealer prep" and "transportation," $900 for an extended warranty (that's only worth $400), etc. Even though John got ripped-off, he probably told all his friends what a shrewd negotiator he is because the dealer paid him $2,000 for his old clunker.

The "payment buyer" gets set up for a similar rip-off. After telling the salesman how much of a monthly payment he can afford, the dealership structures the transaction to wring the maximum amount of profit out of the buyer. The length of the loan is extended, a larger down payment is required, the purchase price of the car is as high as possible, numerous overpriced or worthless options are added, etc. The buyer doesn't even notice that he's been fleeced--he's just happy his payment is "affordable."

"Bait & switch" is a very common trick in the car business. The advertisement describes a great car at a real low price, but when people arrive at the dealer to see it, they're told, "Gee, we're sorry, but that was just sold. However, we do have another car just like it for only a few dollars more." In some cases, the original car in the ad never existed. (This is an illegal business practice.)

"The deposit" scam involves telling people that they have to attach a deposit to their offer on a car. Their deposit check is used to prevent them from leaving after their offer is turned down, giving the salesman more time to wear down his victim. "Gee, I'm sorry, but we can't seem to find your check."

"We can't find your keys" is a scam that works just like the "deposit check." The salesman asks for your car keys "to have your car appraised while we're talking." The keys are "temporarily misplaced" to prevent you from leaving.

"The closer" is typically the best (and highest paid) salesman in a dealership. He'll usually be sent in to replace the first salesman if he's unable to get enough money out of you. Watch out--he's really good. Unless you're very knowledgeable and have nerves of steel, you're no match for this guy. (Get out while you still have the shirt on your back!)

"The bump" or "raise" describes the sales practice of continually coming back to ask for more money. First it's $500 ("Mr. Smith, we're about $1,000 apart on this deal, but we're willing to split the difference with you, is that OK?"), then it's $200 ("Mr. Smith, I'm working real hard to try and get this deal through for you. I think I can talk my boss into it if you can just go up $200.", then $100, etc.

What's particularly outrageous about this practice is that it's probably used the most on people who are already getting a bad deal, even though the salesman claims otherwise. "Gee, Mr. Smith, you're practically stealing this car from us. Please don't tell anyone about the deal you're getting--I wouldn't want word to get out that I'm a pushover." Of course, Mr. Smith is convinced that he's getting a great deal, so he'll tell everyone, which is exactly what the salesman wants him to do.

"Lowballing" is basically an outright lie told to a customer to get him to come in (or come back) to the dealership. This can be done on the phone, quoting someone a low price to get them to come in, then making up an excuse as to why they can't buy a car at that price. "We only had one at that price, and we just sold it. As long as you're here, let me show you a similar car that's only a few dollars more." "I'm sorry we couldn't come down far enough to reach an agreement today, Mr. Jones. We'll be able to lower the price on that car if you come back tomorrow afternoon. I'm sure we'll be able to accept your original offer."

"The four squares" is an old trick, but it works quite well if the victim hasn't seen it before. The salesman takes a sheet of paper and draws two lines, dividing the page into four squares. The salesman then asks how much the buyer would like to pay for the new car, and writes his answer in one of the squares. The amount the buyer would like to receive for his trade-in goes in another square, and the monthly payment the buyer would like goes in the third square. (No matter how ridiculous the buyer's numbers are, they aren't challenged at all (yet).

The buyer is then asked if he would buy the car right there, for those terms. Of course, he says he would, so the salesman has him sign the paper and put up a large deposit. The salesman then takes the "offer" to another room. After a while, he returns, telling the buyer those numbers won't work. The salesman quickly goes to work on the "four-square paper," reducing the trade-in, then increasing the purchase price and the monthly payment while the buyer watches nervously. They negotiate back and forth and the numbers are changed many times. The salesman leaves periodically to "get the manager's approval," then returns to attack the numbers some more. The sheet of paper quickly becomes a jumbled mess, and the buyer is becoming confused. (The plan is working.)

Many other tricks are used by salesmen to confuse buyers so they can't keep track of all the parts of a car deal. As soon as they become confused, the salesmen can then take advantage of them.

When to Buy

At certain times of any given month or year, a salesman or dealer will be more motivated to sell cars for little (or no) profit. Knowing when these times occur, and how motivated the salesmen are, will allow a car buyer to negotiate a lower price.

The end of a model year always offers larger discounts from the sticker price, but there are pitfalls that buyers should be aware of before trying to take advantage of these "bargains." (Be sure to read the section titled, "Year-End Sales.")

Most salesmen work on commission and will be affected by some type of a monthly quota. The benefits of meeting a quota can range anywhere from keeping his job to winning an expensive vacation trip, or getting paid a higher percentage on all the cars he sold during that month. Obviously, if your sale is the one that "puts him over the top," he will benefit greatly even if your deal has little or no profit in it for the dealership. Because of this common practice, you can usually get a better deal during the last 2-3 days of every month.

Dealerships often become eligible for factory-to-dealer cash incentives which lower their cost on specific models. These are not always publicized, and don't expect dealers to inform you when an incentive exists on the car you want (many dealers even withhold this information from their salespeople).

Sometimes dealer incentives are volume-based, meaning the more cars they sell during the incentive period, the more they get for every car sold during that time. Just like the end-of-the-month advantage, you'll usually get a better deal if you buy during the last few days of a volume-based incentive program, especially if a customer rebate program exists at the same time.

To find out when dealer and customer incentive programs begin and end, you'll need to read a Fighting Chance® listing. (See the "Information Sources" section for details.)

How to Negotiate

When you are visiting dealerships, salesmen will swarm around you even though you tell them you're "just looking." Tell them you're not going to buy anything for three or four weeks and they'll usually disappear so you can enjoy looking at different models.

Decide which model you want, or which models you'll settle for if the price is right. Be sure to look up their mechanical track records by checking the April annual car issue of *Consumer Reports*.

You can usually save a lot of money by arranging your own financing, so call your credit union or bank, shop around at other lenders, then decide where you're going to finance your new car. Get your loan pre-approved and do this *before* you begin negotiating on a car. Limit the term to 48 months (or less) and don't borrow more than 80% of the purchase price, or you could end up owing more than the car is worth in one or two years.

Get a current printout from Fighting Chance® listing the factory invoice and all customer rebates and dealer incentives, then figure out what the dealer's actual cost is on the car you want. Subtract the holdback amount and any dealer incentives from the invoice amount; what's left is the dealer's actual cost. Don't include the customer rebate, if any--that's your money. Add $200 to $300 to the dealer's actual cost--that will be the amount of your *initial* offer. (Don't laugh--just read on.)

When you're ready to start negotiating, pick at least two or three dealerships you will give initial offers to, then take your invoice and incentive printouts with you to the dealer. If you can get away with it, try to meet with the fleet manager, but if that doesn't work, pick a salesperson who looks and sounds like someone you can put up with.

Tell the salesman you have decided which car to buy and you are prepared to make an offer. When he asks how you are going to pay for the car, tell him your bank is willing to loan you the money, but you are open to other financing options. Don't give him your driver's license or Social Security numbers, unless you want him to run a quick credit check--they do that so they'll know how much of a monthly payment you can afford, then they'll try every trick in the book to charge you as much as you can afford. Don't fall for it; just tell them it isn't necessary--your credit is good.

Don't show all your cards at once; if you tell him up front that you know all their tricks so he's not going to be able to rip you off, you'll probably make him so mad that you'll never be able to buy a car from him at a reasonable price. Let him think he has the advantage, even though the advantage will be yours if you know the dealer's cost and their tricks. Let him think they might finance your car, and you may get a better price--tell him you'll be willing to discuss financing *after* you've agreed on a price.

Use the same strategy for any trade-in; tell him you'll discuss it afterwards, but count on selling your old car yourself, knowing that a dealer is not going to pay more than wholesale (if that much) unless he's made a fortune on your new car.

Whatever you do, don't give them your old car keys or a "good faith" deposit before you've agreed on a price. An unscrupulous dealer will just use these to hold you hostage while they try to wear you down, claiming that someone has misplaced them so you can't leave.

Never forget that your best negotiating tool is your ability (and willingness) to walk out when they start playing games intended to trick you into paying too much. If you stay, they'll eventually wear you down, and they'll have won the game.

You will usually have to make at least two or three offers at the same dealership before you get a good deal, and you'll have to walk out after they turn down each of the offers to convince them that they're not going to get any more money out of you. Yes, this takes a few visits to the same dealer, but if each visit is a polite "take-it-or-leave-it" offer, instead of a two or three hour battle, it won't take that much time. This is the only way to get the best deal.

After you've presented your initial offer, which is only $200 to $300 above the dealer's cost, the salesman will tell you that they couldn't possibly sell the car for that price because it cost them more than the amount of your offer. Now is the time to pull out your printout from Fighting Chance® and show him that you know exactly what their cost is--$200 to $300 less than the amount of your offer. When you do this, don't have a smirk on your face or a cocky attitude, just calmly show him what the dealer's cost is, including the holdback and any factory incentives. Be prepared for him to challenge the numbers, because he probably didn't know what their cost was until you told him.

Unless it's your lucky day, they're not going to accept your initial offer. (That's OK--it was just part of the plan.) When they reject it, tell *them* to give you a written quote of the exact price they would accept, with the understanding that you are going to make the same offer at four other dealers. The dealer with the lowest bid will be the one who sells you the car. Then tell the salesman that you have another appointment, and you can only wait ten minutes for him to return with their bid. When you have the bid (or their time runs out because they're stalling), leave the dealership immediately and repeat the process at several others.

> Incidentally, if they refuse to negotiate on your terms, tell them you're sure you can find someone else who will, then thank them for their time and leave. Be polite, because you want them to change their mind and call you back.
>
> What usually happens when you walk out after rejecting one of their offers is that they will run after you, often waiting until you're at the edge of the lot (or at your car) to see if you're bluffing. They need to get you back inside or they won't be able to sell you anything. When they try this, tell them you're not going back inside unless they're ready to accept your offer. If necessary, give them your phone number and tell them to call you when they're serious about selling the car. Remind them that you are going to several other dealers to make the same offer, then leave.

When you have as many competing bids as you want, call the dealers with the high bids and tell them what the low bid was, then ask if they will beat that bid to sell you the car. They probably won't offer to beat it by more than a token amount (maybe as little as $25 or $50), but that's OK because you're not going to offer that much, unless the low bids are so close to your revised target price that you're willing to accept one of them. The one with the lowest bid after you've given all of them a second chance *on the phone* will be the one you return to for your second written offer to purchase.

Before you make your second written offer, determine your revised target price. This should be an amount that only allows the dealer a $400 to $600 profit, depending on the price range of the car. In some cases, this would be at or near the factory invoice, leaving the dealer with the holdback money for his profit. However, if there's a factory-to-dealer cash incentive involved, you should try to get all of the incentive, which means you'll be buying for hundreds (or maybe thousands) of dollars below the factory invoice. Settle for half of the incentive money later, if that's the best you can do.

Present the second offer in the same manner as the first, asking for a written counteroffer if your offer is rejected. Remind them that you will be making the same offer at several other dealers who had low bids. Then leave. Don't let them talk you into raising your offer while you're there--there's a much better chance that they'll cave in first if you walk out after your offer is rejected. Stay in control and you'll win.

As you start offering dealers $400 to $600 over cost, they may worry that one of the others might accept your offer, so don't be too quick to offer more than that until several weeks have gone by and there aren't any takers. If that happens, call them back and ask if they've reconsidered your offer. If there's still no interest, raise your target price by $200 to $300 and repeat the written offer procedure until you get the deal you want.

Unless you're in a seller's market, you should be able to find a dealer who's tempted by one of your offers. In a booming seller's market, when inventories are low and most of the dealers aren't undercutting each other, you may end up paying 2% to 4% over factory invoice, especially if you're not willing to wait several months for another incentive program to come along.

When you've reached an agreement on price, they'll want to discuss financing, trade-in, and the usual array of "after-sell" rip-offs. If you've done your homework, and stand your ground, they won't be able to take advantage of you. (This means you'll probably use your own lender, sell your own car, and refuse to pay for anything other than tax, license, and destination charge.)

Since they didn't make much on the car, they may try to make up for it on the back-end. If they claim that you have to pay for one or more items on the "second sticker" because they're already on the car, tell them to take them off or get you another car, because you don't want them and you're not going to pay for them. Let them know you'll cancel the purchase if they insist on charging you for unwanted or worthless "options." (For more information, see "Tricks Salesmen Use," "Back-End Sales," and "Charges You Don't Have to Pay.")

Before you take delivery of your new car, be sure to give it a thorough inspection. Look for dents, scratches, flaws in the paint, poor fit or finish, upholstery defects, etc. Make sure all lights and accessories function properly, then test drive the car. Make a list of things that need to be fixed, keep a copy for yourself, then have the dealership fix everything *before* you take delivery. You'll have a much better chance of getting things fixed to your satisfaction before you actually buy the car.

Charges You Don't Have to Pay
& The Ones You Do

Many charges that a dealer will add onto the sticker or the contract are nothing but additional profit. Classic examples of this include: Additional Dealer Markup (ADM), Additional Dealer Profit (ADP), or Additional Market Value (AMV). This is pure and simple extra profit--don't pay it.

Watch out for the "second sticker" (put on by the dealer) next to the manufacturer's sticker. This is where a lot of unnecessary, overpriced, or worthless "options" are added onto the sticker to inflate the profit margin. Examples: fabric protection, paint sealer, rustproofing/under-coating, pinstriping, "special value package," "protection package," floor mats, etc. Don't pay for any of these.

Two very common rip-offs are "dealer preparation" (or "dealer prep") and "national advertising" charges; you don't have to pay these--they're already included in the factory invoice. Some dealers will also try to add on a 1-2% charge for their local advertising. Don't pay it--that's part of the cost of doing business. (You wouldn't want to pay extra for "building electricity charges" or "employee benefit charges," so don't pay extra for their advertising, either.)

Watch for items listed as "processing charges" or "closing costs." What they're trying to do is make you pay for their employees handling the paperwork. A $10 or $15 "DMV title fee" may be justified, but watch out for a $100 (or more) paperwork processing charge--don't pay it.

If the dealer is handling the financing, he'll probably try to sell you credit life or disability insurance. Don't fall for this--if you really need it (and you probably don't) you can always buy it from your own insurance agent for a lot less.

The list of items you do have to pay for is fairly short: the destination/freight charge, sales tax, DMV license fees, and the car itself.

"One-Price" & "No-Haggle" Deals

You've probably seen manufacturers and dealers advertising "one-price" or "no-haggle" deals on new cars, and if you're like most people, it may have sounded like a pretty good deal. Well, people may like it because they hate to "haggle," but the dealers are usually the ones who benefit the most because they end up with a higher profit on each car than they would get in normal competition.

In spite of all the popularity and success of the Saturn, a serious shopper can buy a comparable car from another manufacturer for at least $1,000 less than he would pay for a Saturn with similar equipment. The reason for the price difference is that Saturn dealers are making a lot more money on each and every car. The lowest-priced Saturn model with no options or add-ons still makes $1287 profit for the dealer. Higher-priced models, especially those with options, can generate profits exceeding $2,000 per car.

At the present time, Saturn dealers have the only true no-haggle (non-negotiable) prices on all of their cars. Other manufacturers have offered one-price deals on occasion to reduce inventories, but these are not always non-negotiable prices. For example, all Ford Escorts are supposed to have the same low price, but many dealers have lowered prices to sell more cars. GM's "California Value Pricing" program has one-price deals on 46 specially-equipped 1994 models, at supposedly non-negotiable prices. Only time will tell if they really are non-negotiable.

Year-End Sales:
Buying Last Year's Model

Some car buyers like to wait until the new models arrive, then they purchase last year's model during a dealer's "big year-end sale." While it is true that they are getting a "brand new car" at a reduced price, they're also buying a car that is already one year old and has probably depreciated several thousand dollars before they even get to drive it home. If that fact doesn't bother you, and you still prefer to buy last year's model, there a few things you should know before buying one.

The best year-end deals can usually be found on cars that have a manufacturers "carryover allowance," which is an amount the dealer receives for every previous year model vehicle left on his lot when the new models arrive. GM and Ford carryover allowances are the most common, and are usually 5% of the MSRP (sticker). Some imports have a specific dollar amount, which could be as much as $6,000 to $10,000 on a luxury car.

Here's an example of how a carryover can affect the actual dealer's cost on a domestic car: On a typical $20,000 car, the dealer would get back an additional $1,000 (carryover) along with the usual holdback ($600 at 3%) and any factory-to-dealer incentives (we'll use $1,000), adding up to $2,600 off the dealer's cost. (Don't forget--none of this will be mentioned on the factory invoice.) Subtract the $2,600 from a typical factory invoice of $16,500 (on a $20,000 car), and you'll see that the dealer's actual cost on the car is only $13,900.

Now the dealer may not be willing to sell the car at his cost, but keep in mind that it is last year's model, and if he can't find another buyer at that price, he'll be forced to sell it below cost. So offer to buy it for his actual cost ($13,900 in our example) and see what happens. If that doesn't work, offer to let him keep some (or all) of the holdback money (which means raising your offer as high as $14,500). Don't go much higher, or you'll end up paying more than the car is worth. Remember--it's already a year old, so it's depreciated several thousand dollars, and it was only "worth" about $17,000 when it was new.

As you can see, there is the possibility of huge discounts on year-end models, so make sure you receive them if you plan on buying a car this way. Don't settle for less, or you'll end up losing a lot of money if you sell the car or trade it in within several years.

To find out which manufacturers use carryover allowances, and how much they are, consumers need to use one of the services that track this information (listed under "Information Sources").

Auto Brokers

Auto brokers and car buying services both claim to be able to save you big money on the purchase of a new vehicle, as their advertising and endorsements mention, but there are major differences in how they operate and make their money. These differences, however, are significant and could affect not only the price you pay for a car, but what kind of service you receive after the purchase.

Auto brokers have been around for a long time, but they don't appear to have captured much of the car-buying market. How they operate could be at least partially responsible for their lack of popularity. Brokers take orders from consumers, buy the cars from dealers (with the broker actually taking title to the vehicles), then they sell the cars to consumers. Because of this, the broker actually becomes the "original owner" of the car.

Instead of receiving a fixed payment for negotiating a purchase, brokers make differing amounts of money based on the spread between what they pay for a car and what they sell it for. The broker's desire to make a bigger profit is in direct conflict with the consumer's desire to get the lowest possible price, and since a broker is actually taking title and delivery of every vehicle he handles, he would have to make more money on a car than someone who is just doing the negotiating.

One drawback to using an auto broker concerns their taking title to a car before they sell it to the consumer, which makes the broker the "original owner" of record with the manufacturer (just as a leasing company would be). In some cases, this can result in "less than great" service if you take your car to a dealership that treats people better if they bought a car there, and worse yet, if they resent the fact that you used an auto broker.

Another drawback, which could be a serious problem, is that vehicle recall notices are usually sent only to the original owner, so if they don't get forwarded, you may not find out that your car was recalled for a safety defect.

Car Buying Services

Numerous car buying services have sprung up recently and are gaining in popularity. For a fee (usually $100 to $150), these services promise to save you money by doing the negotiating for you. Most of them even offer a money-back guarantee that they can get you a better deal than you could get on your own.

Car buying services don't resell cars; all they do is represent you as a professional car buyer, then give you all the bids they've received on the car you want. When they're through collecting bids from dealerships (usually at least five), they turn the bids over to you to decide which dealer you want to use. The bids are usually from local dealerships, unless you specify how far you're willing to drive to save more money.

All that's left for you to do after you've selected a dealer is to decide whether you want to arrange your own financing (which you'll do if you want to save money) or use the dealer's financing. Then you simply go to the dealer to sign the papers and pick up your new car.

There are many advantages to using a car buying service over an auto broker. Most people will end up getting their new car from a local dealership (after the buying service has negotiated a low price), so they should be treated just like anyone else who bought a car there if they need to go back later for service. (This is an added benefit for people who are concerned about it.) Also, since no one else is taking title to the car and reselling it, the consumer will be registered as the "original owner," ensuring that he will receive any recall notices pertaining to his car.

Car buying services only negotiate prices, they don't take title or delivery on new cars, so their overhead should be lower than that of an auto broker who actually buys the car and takes possession. An auto broker obviously needs to make more money on each car to cover the additional costs.

Not all car buying services are alike--some protect their customers from "back-end sales" and some don't. If they don't, you may be in for a surprise when you go to pick up your car. One major buying service is part of a "club" that offers its members discount coupons for service at a number of national auto repair chains. Several of those chains have had numerous undercover busts for selling unnecessary repairs. (These companies, and their undercover busts, are described in other chapters of this book.)

If you don't have the ability (or the desire) to negotiate on a new car, you should definitely use a car buying service. The service that I think does the best job at protecting consumers, and working hard to find them the best deal, is the ConsumerWise® Car Club of San Francisco, California. Unlike most other services that only get four or five bids, the Car Club will keep negotiating (or shopping around) until they find a good deal. Their fee is only $89 and they have a money-back guarantee that you can't find a better deal. For information, call toll-free 1-800-CAR-CLUB.

Leasing: Good Deal or Bad?

Auto leasing seems to be gaining in popularity, in part because of manufacturer and dealer advertising. Leasing enables someone to drive a more expensive car than they would normally be able to buy, due to lower down payments and monthly payments than a typical car loan. This may be very tempting to someone who buys a new car every two to three years, especially if they don't want to tie up a lot of cash in their car.

The reason lease payments are so low is that the lessee (consumer) is not paying off the car--he's just "renting" it for a specified period of time, usually three years. The lease payment only covers the depreciation for the term of the lease, interest, and a profit made by the leasing company and/or dealer.

At the end of a typical lease, the lessee will not have any equity in the car. If he wants to keep it at that point, he'll have to come up with a lump sum usually equal to the wholesale value of the car. If he doesn't want the car, he can just return it to the leasing company, owing nothing, provided the car is in good shape and has accumulated less than 15,000 miles per year.

There are several major drawbacks to leasing a car, the foremost being that it's more expensive than a normal car loan if you end up purchasing the car at the end of the lease. If you don't buy the car, and you just lease another new one, you'll never stop making car payments, and you'll never have any equity in your car.

Qualifying for an auto lease can be more difficult than a normal loan because of the lower down payment. The low down payment also means that you can't usually get out of a lease early without losing your shirt.

Another potentially serious drawback in leasing is that the leasing company is the "original owner" of record. This means that all safety recall notices would go to the leasing company, not you, so if they fail to forward the notices, you may not find out that your car was recalled.

211

If you decide to lease a car, make sure you shop around and negotiate as you would if you were purchasing. Your cap reduction and monthly payments will be higher if the lease is based on the MSRP (sticker), so get the cap cost as close to dealer invoice as possible. ("Capital or cap reduction" is the down payment; "capital or cap cost" is the purchase price of the car.)

Look for factory-subsidized leases; they're often at rates so low that leasing could actually be a good deal. This is usually done to reduce bloated inventories of unsold cars. Unfortunately, in many cases the low-interest leases specify "based on MSRP," so buyers are not allowed to negotiate a lower price on the car.

One last tip: Don't let on that you're going to lease the car until after you've negotiated a low price. Dealers (and leasing companies) love doing leases based on the MSRP because they make a lot more money, so don't tell them. When they ask how you're going to pay for it, just tell them you'll arrange your own financing later.

Information Sources:
Factory Invoice/Rebates/Incentives
& Car Buying Service

A number of small paperback books listing factory invoice prices (along with the MSRP) can be found in most libraries and bookstores. They're known as "new car price guides" and they usually sell for about five dollars. Unfortunately, they don't have information on rebates or incentives.

The most comprehensive service for new car information is Fighting Chance® of Long Beach, California. For only $19.95 the Fighting Chance® package provides specific information on new car market conditions, negotiating tactics, factory invoice prices, customer rebates, and factory-to-dealer cash incentives to help you get the lowest price on a new car. This is the only service I've found with current information on dealer incentives--it's updated every two weeks. Their toll-free number is 1-800-288-1134.

If you hate the thought of negotiating for a new car, but would still like to save money, you should use a car buying service. The one I recommend is the Consumer-Wise® Car Club (see the preceding section for details). The Car Club can also provide immediate information on factory invoice prices for $9.95, but this does not include information on rebates, holdbacks, or factory-to-dealer cash incentives. For information, call toll-free 1-800-CAR-CLUB.

Tips for Used Car Buyers

To avoid paying too much on a used car or truck, be sure to check several local newspapers to compare prices on similar vehicles. Most bookstores (and libraries) carry inexpensive paperbacks listing used car prices, but those are merely estimates. What a particular car is worth depends more on its condition compared to similar cars for sale in that area and, of course, what people are willing to pay for them.

When buying from a private party, unless the vehicle is still covered by the factory warranty, you'll be buying the vehicle "as is." This means no warranty at all. So, unless you're an experienced auto mechanic, don't ever buy a used car without having *your* mechanic give it a thorough inspection before you sign any contracts or pay any money. You'll have to pay for the inspection, but it's money well-spent, and any problems that are discovered can often be used to negotiate a lower price.

Beware of promises that aren't put in writing. Verbal

statements concerning a car's condition (or any warranties) are almost always worthless--if someone won't put it in writing, they probably have no intention of honoring it, and you won't be able to enforce it.

If you are considering the purchase of a used vehicle from a car dealer, keep in mind that many dealers make more money on a used car than a new one, simply because it's much easier for consumers to find out what the dealer's cost is on a new car. The higher the price, the bigger the profit margin, so don't be afraid to offer a lot less than the asking price. It's not unusual for a dealer to make $2,000 to $3,000 profit on a used car selling for $10,000 so there's plenty of room to negotiate.

Most dealers sell their used cars "as is" (without any warranty), and they're not usually very cooperative when it comes to letting people take their vehicles to other shops for prepurchase inspections. Of course, they'll have lots of excuses for those policies. Here are several examples (which are often untrue): "That's not necessary, our mechanics have already done a thorough inspection." "All of our cars are completely safety-checked. They wouldn't be on our lot if they needed any repairs."

While it may be true that a dealer's cars have been "safety-checked" so you're not going to have a steering or brake failure on the way home from the dealership, I seriously doubt that their inspections are very thorough, or done with full disclosure. I've heard too many horror stories from used car buyers to believe otherwise.

You can take advantage of a dealer's reluctance to have his cars inspected by insisting on a warranty. Even though all the used cars on a dealer's lot may have "as is" stickers on the windows, don't forget that practically everything is negotiable when you're buying a car. Tell the salesman, "If the car's condition is as good as you say it is, you shouldn't have any problem giving me a written, bumper-to-bumper six month warranty." (Ask for six months, settle for three if that's the best deal you can get.)

At this point, the salesman will probably tell you they can't do that (which isn't usually true) and counter with a suggestion that you should buy an extended warranty (for $800 to $1200) if you're so concerned with future repair costs. Extended warranties are negotiable, and they only cost the dealer 30-40% of the amount most people pay for them, so tell the salesman he's going to have to thrown in the warranty, or you're not going to buy the car.

Here's where you'll probably have to use your "best negotiating weapon" if he says he can't give you any kind of warranty--get up, tell him you're going to find another dealer who's more cooperative, then leave. If he really wants to sell you a car, he'll stop you at the front door, or maybe at the door to your car. Don't let him string you along by promising that "he'll see what he can do"--tell him to throw in the warranty, or you're leaving.

To get the best deal on a car, you'll probably have to terminate the negotiations and walk out at least once before you get what you want. This is often the best way for you to remain in control; if the salesman stays in control, you'll pay too much for the car.

When you start to leave, the salesman may tell you that the price he quoted is only good for that day, and if you come back later, you'll have to pay more for the same car. Your comeback for this line should be: "That's too bad. If you really mean it, I guess I'll have to buy a car from someone else when I'm ready."

Several concluding tips: Know what a car is worth before you decide to buy it. Don't be afraid to walk out if the salesman is playing games, especially if he keeps trying to "bump" the price up. Insist that he treat you with respect and honesty. Unless a dealer lets you get a pre-purchase inspection, don't buy a used car from him without some kind of free or low-priced written warranty. If you're buying a used car from a private party, make sure you have *your* mechanic check the car thoroughly *before* you buy it.

CHAPTER 18

Blackmail, Censorship,
or Business as Usual?

Why is it that so many consumers never hear about the tricks used by car salesmen to make huge profits? Is it because few people know the inside secrets and fewer still are willing to tell the public what they know? Or is it because a serious effort is made to prevent the truth from getting out?

An article I found in the April '92 issue of *Consumer Reports* suggests that the last question is closer to the truth. The article was titled, "Are automobile dealers editing your local newspaper?" and it details the pressure car dealers often put on newspapers to keep them from printing anything dealers may consider "unfavorable."

The *Consumer Reports* article gave specific examples of newspapers that printed wire-service stories on how to bargain when buying a car. A barrage of car dealer complaints on the "lucky" newspapers resulted in an unofficial policy to avoid similar articles in the future. The unlucky newspapers were punished by car dealers who pulled their ads; some papers lost all of their auto advertising for up to six months, until the papers apologized for running the "offending" stories.

Were these just a few isolated incidents, or examples

of common practices in the media? To find out, *Consumer Reports* conducted a random survey of 50 daily newspapers, asking editors and writers if local car dealers had any effect on the news. About one-third of the journalists in the survey admitted that they wouldn't run stories on car-buying due to actual (or anticipated) dealer complaints.

One syndicated columnist recently told me that any articles on "how to save money when buying a new car" would only be printed in 50-60% of the papers carrying the column. Another columnist said that any articles car dealers might see as "unfriendly" had to be very carefully worded or most papers wouldn't print them.

ATTEMPTS TO SUPPRESS THIS INFO--

I have experienced similar "censorship" in radio and newspapers while spreading the word about the first edition of this book. Although many radio stations have let me do interviews, a significant percentage of them would not allow me to name the well-known auto repair companies that had been charged with fraudulent business practices. Why not? Because they were advertisers.

My show ("Shop Talk") was cancelled on one radio station after mentioning a national auto repair chain that had a number of undercover busts. Why? Because a shop from that very chain was a major advertiser on the station. (Since then, that same company has been accused of selling unnecessary repairs following undercover investigations in two more states.)

Newspaper editors have asked me to write articles on auto repair, but wouldn't allow me to include names of companies that were charged with fraudulent business practices after undercover investigations. Why not? Because many of them were advertisers.

It should be obvious by now why so many people never learn "what auto mechanics and car salesmen don't want you to know"--the information is not allowed in many newspapers, or on many radio and TV stations.

Speaking of television, why haven't we ever seen a good undercover investigation of a major auto repair chain on "Prime Time Live," "60 Minutes," "20/20," or "Inside Edition"? Several local stations have caught the same major company in the (alleged) sale of unnecessary repairs in two different states, and the practices that got Sears in trouble were commonly used by other companies as well (based on an investigation by the New York Attorney General's office). All I've seen on national TV is an undercover investigation of several small repair shops and gas stations, who obviously would never advertise on a TV network.

Until many radio stations, TV stations, and newspapers develop the integrity and backbone required to stand up to automotive advertisers, the advertisers will continue to get away with keeping "unfavorable" information out of the public eye. Because many consumers won't learn how to protect themselves, they'll continue to be victimized by incompetent or dishonest repair shops and overcharged by "slick" car salesmen.

THE SOLUTION--

As you can imagine, there will be many attempts to keep the auto repair and car-buying secrets in this book from becoming common knowledge. So do your friends a favor--if you think this information will save them money, tell them about it.

CHAPTER 19

Are Chain Stores
Cleaning Up Their Act?

The 1992 charges of fraudulent business practices following undercover investigations at Sears Auto Centers sent
shock waves throughout the entire repair industry. Auto
service sales at Sears fell 23% after the charges hit the
news, and business also dropped off at many unrelated repair shops across the country. Consumers postponed as
much auto maintenance and service as possible, with
many expressing the fear that "if you can't trust Sears,
who can you trust?"

Public trust in auto mechanics was never very high,
but the Sears scandal in California seemed to drive it even
lower. Statements made by company officials in defense
of their "recommending replacement of (worn) parts before they fail," then claiming that was an "accepted industry practice" didn't help Sears at all, because the parts replaced on the undercover cars were already in perfect
condition. This just created more consumer distrust in the
repair industry.

An investigation of auto repair practices by the New
York Attorney General's office was not publicized, fortunately for Sears, because it probably would have scared
consumers even more and made it more difficult for Sears

to regain the public's trust.

The New York investigation revealed problems far worse than those uncovered at Sears in California, including the widespread employment of service advisors with little or no previous training or experience in auto repair. In spite of their obvious lack of qualifications, their job description included inspecting and diagnosing vehicles prior to making service and repair recommendations to consumers.

At the Sears centers, the principal function of the service advisors was to generate sales of auto repair services and products. Their pay was based on an incentive compensation plan consisting of a minimal base salary plus commission that was tied directly to their total sales, so the more they sold, the more they were paid. In addition, the company ran contests to see who could produce the biggest increase in sales for specific parts or services.

The New York Attorney General claimed that unnecessary repairs were sold at Sears as a direct result of their "incentive compensation and goal-setting program," and that Sears service advisors often refused to honor lifetime service contracts they had sold for wheel alignments and other services, unless vehicle owners agreed to pay for additional repairs.

According to the Attorney General, the practices found at Sears were not limited to its auto centers in New York, but were being used nationwide, and by other companies as well.

U.S. SENATE SUBCOMMITTEE--
FOCUS ON AUTO REPAIR CHAINS

As a result of the Sears bust in June, and statements made regarding "common practices" such as sales incentive programs, commissions, contests, and quotas on specific parts, the U.S. Senate Commerce Committee called a Consumer subcommittee hearing one month later to look into practices at repair shops operated by chains.

At the hearing, the Maryland Attorney General called for an amendment to a federal law to make franchisers legally responsible for deceptive or fraudulent practices by their franchisees. He said auto repair franchisers have no economic incentive to discourage fraudulent practices, because franchisers profit from all business activity at their stores, whether they're honest or not.

The Attorney General told of a 1986-87 investigation done by his office that found a pattern of fraudulent business practices at 11 out of 13 Cottman Transmission Systems, Inc. shops in Maryland. A state court ordered Cottman to pay a $100,000 fine, but the issue of restitution is still in litigation. (The 14 state Aamco Transmission investigation was also done in 1986-87, revealing a more widespread pattern of fraudulent practices.)

Other reform proposals presented at the hearing included licensing of repair shops, setting minimum standards for certification of mechanics, holding parent companies to strict standards of liability, and eliminating the commission-based sales structure.

COMMISSION-BASED PAY

"Commission-based sales" was listed as a problem area because Sears had been using it to determine the earnings of its service advisors, and a number of people in the industry tried to defend its use by claiming that it was a common practice. (That wasn't true--it was only a common practice at chain stores, not at independent shops.)

Instead of paying mechanics or service advisors a salary or hourly wage based on their knowledge or experience, commission-based pay usually involves a minimal salary plus a sales commission which often represents 30-50% (or more) of the worker's total earnings. Some franchise chain stores have been found to pay their mechanics a straight commission based on everything they sell and install, with no base salary. The danger of these practices should be obvious: employees have to sell a lot of parts and services just to earn a living, and this often results in the sale of unnecessary repairs.

Since the Senate hearing, a number of company-owned Goodyear service centers in two states have been accused of selling unnecessary repairs after undercover investigations were done. In both cases, mechanics working in the shops told of commission-based pay and pressure from management to increase sales.

Sears discontinued its sales incentive program several weeks after the investigation became a major news item. Goodyear waited until four months after its second state investigation to announce that it would discontinue its commission-based pay for mechanics working in 900 company-owned stores. (However, the 700 franchises and 2300 Goodyear-affiliate stores are free to use any type of pay structure for their employees, including commission, because they are independently owned and operated.)

NAAG AUTO REPAIR TASK FORCE

Another outcome of the Sears scandal was creation of the National Association of Attorneys General (NAAG) automotive repair task force, which was set up to protect consumers and address problem areas in the repair industry. Training, communication, and standards in compensation and ethics were stressed by the task force as its goals for the industry. The task force also encouraged companies to share their business practices with NAAG.

Several task force hearings have already been held, giving interested parties a chance to explain, criticize, or defend repair practices in the industry, and to offer solutions to perceived problems. A report containing the findings of the task force is scheduled to be released in the fall of 1994.

Major topics of the hearings were ethics, lack of training (incompetence), and commission-based pay for mechanics and service advisors. (The subject of commission-based pay keeps coming up because even though chain stores claim that it is a common practice, many automotive professionals see it as a cancer that has infected the industry.)

MAINTENANCE AWARENESS PROGRAM (THE CHAIN STORES' SOLUTION)

Established as an industry-wide coalition of auto repair companies and trade associations, the Maintenance Awareness Program (MAP) was designed to improve consumer confidence in the repair industry after the Sears scandal. MAP represents the majority of the nation's multi-bay retail automotive outlets (i.e., chain stores), independent service stations, suppliers, manufacturers, industry associations and publications; it was founded by the Automotive Parts & Accessories Association (AAPA) and Sears.

Initial goals of MAP include developing uniform inspection procedures, a code of ethics, standards of service, and preventive maintenance recommendations. Long-term goals include upgrading the skill levels of technicians and service writers, improving the public image of professional technicians, and giving recognition to outstanding individuals.

To achieve MAP's objectives, the following committees were formed: Uniform Inspection Guidelines, Consumer Education, Proactive Issues/Liaison, Consumer Preventive Maintenance, Image Enhancement of the Industry Professional, and Service Provider Committee.

The Service Provider Committee has already developed the Pledge to Customers, a promise to consumers that the company and its personnel are ethical professionals; and the Standards of Service, to help consumers understand why technicians recommend specific services for their vehicles.

> Contained in the code of ethics developed by the MAP committee are requirements that repair shops:
> 1) recommend service based on system failure, preventive maintenance, or improved performance and clearly explain service needs to the consumer; 2) train and hire qualified personnel; 3) provide a written estimate and not perform any work without the customer's permission; and 4) include a written limited warranty at no charge.

MAP's Proactive Issues/Liaison Committee has established working relationships with several regulatory groups, including the NAAG Task Force and the California Bureau of Automotive Repair (BAR).

Representatives from both groups spoke to MAP members in 1993. The former head of the NAAG Task Force told members that the task force "is not your enemy" and encouraged cooperation in addressing problems in the industry. The California BAR chief told members that his agency gets 60,000 auto repair complaints every year, most of them due to dishonesty, incompetence, and incorrect paperwork.

COMPANY POLICIES & CHANGES--

Note: The initial company practices and/or changes in policy may not apply to franchise stores in the following chains. Franchises are independently owned and operated, so owners are free to use any form of compensation they desire, including commission and other sales incentives.

Goodyear Auto Centers
Practices at company-owned stores: Mechanics previously paid salary plus commission on parts and services, sales contests. Mechanics' commission discontinued June, 1994 after two recent investigations; increased salary instead. Announced new "customer trust program" consisting of three levels of service customers may choose from: "basic level" provides only the service requested; "standard level" includes a free vehicle inspection with requested service, but no additional service unless requested; "premium level" allows the service technician to check and care for complete vehicle needs, but customers still must authorize any repairs. (900 company-owned stores, 700 franchises, 2300 Goodyear-affiliates)

Sears Auto Centers
Major changes after 1992 investigations: discontinued incentive compensation and goal-setting program; no service advisors anymore; "customer service consultants" (salespersons) on salary plus commission for tires, batteries, and shocks only (no commission on repairs); mechanics on salary only, make all repair recommendations; discontinued all oil changes, tune-ups, air conditioning, electrical, and engine work. Safeguards: "mystery shoppers" used for internal undercover checks on store practices. (774 company-owned auto centers)

Winston Tire Company
Major changes in 1992 (during California investigation): Sales commission for store management discontinued, hourly wage or salary instead; discontinued sales contests; mechanics' pay based on hourly wage plus production. Safeguards: random undercover "shopping" by independent company, mechanics must save all replaced parts for review by management, toll-free customer hotline to company headquarters. (165 company-owned stores)

Pep Boys Manny Moe and Jack
Mechanics paid hourly wage up to 1992, changed to commission for less than one year. Mechanics' commission discontinued due to Sears investigation in 1992; pay based on flat rate (specific amount per job) since April, 1993; no commission or sales incentives for mechanics. Service managers paid salary plus commission until 1991; since April, 1991 managers receive salary plus bonus based on customer satisfaction, no quotas or sales incentives. (387 company-owned stores)

Midas Muffler & Brake Shops
Discontinued "price advertising" in 1992; still advertise free brake inspections. Company "discourages payment of sales commission for any shop personnel." However, many franchises use commission to pay their mechanics. (120 company-owned stores, 1700 franchises)

Montgomery Ward Auto Express
Major changes in 1989: mechanics no longer on commission, on salary instead; sales associates no longer initiate repair recommendations, done by qualified mechanics only (in writing); sales associates receive commission; monthly goals for store revenue; store managers receive salary plus bonuses based on customer satisfaction and

store revenue. Safeguards: "Mystery shoppers" used for frequent internal undercover checks on store practices, customer satisfaction surveys and "Bill of Rights."
(362 auto centers)

Firestone Tire & Service Centers
Practices at company-owned stores: Mechanics pay based on flat rate (specific amount per job) since 1987; sales associates paid hourly, managers are salaried; no commissions or sales incentive programs for mechanics, sales associates, or store managers; no monthly quotas. Safeguards: "Mystery shopper" program, toll-free customer complaint line, unannounced store audits.
(1500 company-owned stores, 500 franchises)

CLEANING UP THEIR ACT--
ARE CHAIN STORES SINCERE?

The purpose of the Maintenance Awareness Program was to improve consumer confidence in the industry after the Sears scandal, which caused a drop in business not only at Sears, but at many other companies as well.

It's ironic that some (or many?) of the very companies that are directly responsible for the public's lack of confidence in the repair industry are now banding together to "set new ethical and professional standards for the industry to follow." Their "common practices" of sales commissions, incentive compensation programs, contests, and quotas are responsible for the widespread sale of unnecessary repairs, the undercover investigations, and the loss of revenue due to consumer distrust.

Many companies are complaining about the low skill levels of their mechanics, and sometimes blaming them after their shops get caught in undercover investigations, when the companies are to blame for refusing to pay what the market demands for expert technicians. To make matters worse, by rewarding their mechanics for being better salesmen instead of smarter mechanics, they have little incentive to put in the many hours of training that is necessary to become (and remain) experts. This is why so many of them are known in the industry as "parts changers" instead of professional technicians.

On the subject of mechanics, several cynics have suggested that maybe the chain stores don't want to hire the best ones they can find, because it's a lot easier to train the unexperienced to sell a lot of parts that may not be necessary. After all, chain stores are essentially "mass merchandisers" set up to sell as much merchandise (in this case, auto parts) as possible. Having vehicle inspection sheets and written guidelines that emphasize "recommended (optional) repairs" based on what is claimed to be "industry standards" can be used as an excuse to sell unnecessary repairs under the guise of "preventive maintenance."

Some of the chain stores sound sincere about setting high ethical standards and implementing them. However, several companies never appeared overly concerned in the past when a number of their franchises were charged with fraudulent business practices, at least not sufficiently concerned to do anything about it. In addition, I was disappointed to learn that two of the companies (Goodyear and Midas) with representatives on the committee that developed the MAP code of ethics had a number of shops under investigation while their committee was working on "setting new ethical and professional standards for the industry to follow."

Only time will tell if the Maintenance Awareness Program will really bring higher levels of ethics and professionalism to the industry. In theory, it sounds like a great idea, but it will require many repair shops across the country to conduct business in a totally different manner, which may result in some shops and mechanics making less money than before. Are chain stores sincere about cleaning up their act, or will the desire to increase sales and profits become too great? I guess we'll just have to wait and see.

A CHALLENGE FOR CHAIN STORES--

If discontinuing incentive compensation programs (sales commissions, etc.) and training or hiring better technicians are good ideas for company stores to regain the public's trust, why not do the same thing at franchise stores?

Second Printing Addendum

A consumer fraud lawsuit against Kmart Auto Centers was certified as a class action in August, 1994.

In October of 1994, a similar lawsuit was filed against Goodyear Tire & Rubber Co. over alleged practices at its company-owned auto centers.

Summary

I hope this book didn't leave the impression that people will get ripped-off no matter where they go, because I don't believe that's true. There are many honest, professional repair shops in the country, but consumers must learn how to find them because they're not as visible as many shops that should be avoided.

Beware of low-priced repair shops, especially ones that advertise heavily (this is often a tip-off that you're dealing with mechanics and/or service writers working "on commission"). The victims of the scams detailed in this book had one thing in common--they were all lured by ads for low-priced repairs and/or free inspections. Don't forget: "If it looks too good to be true, it probably is."

I'm not suggesting that *all* shops advertising low-priced repairs or free inspections are dishonest, or that they routinely sell unnecessary repairs. More of them are probably incompetent than dishonest, which is another good reason to avoid them.

After reading the stories in this book, it should be obvious that consumers run a much greater risk of becoming victims if they take their vehicles to different repair shops because they have the lowest prices. To prevent this from happening to you, use the guidelines in this book to find a

233

reputable shop that employs well-trained, highly-skilled technicians who aren't paid a sales commission. The best place to look is usually in large independent repair shops.

For your protection, always remember to:
1. Check out a shop and its mechanics *before* taking your vehicle in for repairs.
2. Get a detailed, written estimate before any work is started. Make sure the problem or symptom that you want diagnosed/repaired is written on the original estimate.
3. Request that all replaced parts be returned to you.
4. For major repairs, get a second (or third) opinion before you authorize any work.